THE SPIRIT
OF MAN

THE SPIRIT
OF MAN

Dr. Ana Méndez Ferrell

Voice of The Light Ministries

Voice Of The Light Ministries

The Spirit of Man

© Dr. Ana Méndez Ferrell

1st English Edition August 2015

Original Title: El Espíritu Del Hombre

All Scripture references are from the New King James Version® (NKJV). Copyright © 1982 by Thomas Nelson. Used by permission. All rights reserved. In some cases from the Amplified® Bible (AMP), Copyright © 1954, 1958, 1962, 1964, 1965, 1987 by The Lockman Foundation (www.lockman.org) unless otherwise noted.

Category:	Deliverance
Publisher:	Voice of The Light Ministries
	P.O. Box 3418
	Ponte Vedra, Florida, 32004
	United States of America
	Telephone: +1.904.834.2447
Printed in:	United States of America
	www.voiceofthelight.com
Paperback ISBN:	**978-1-933163-02-4**
Hardcover ISBN:	**978-1-933163-33-8**

DEDICATION

First of all, I dedicate this book to my Heavenly Father, to my Lord Jesus Christ and to the precious Holy Spirit who revealed to me all that is written here.

Also, I dedicate this to my children, Ana, Pedro, Jordan, and to my beloved daughter-in-law Karen and my grandchildren, Karem and Leon. They represent the new generation who, more than any other, will be filled with the knowledge of God, and to whom God is already preparing to impart a profound revelation of His Spirit and His power to impact the world.

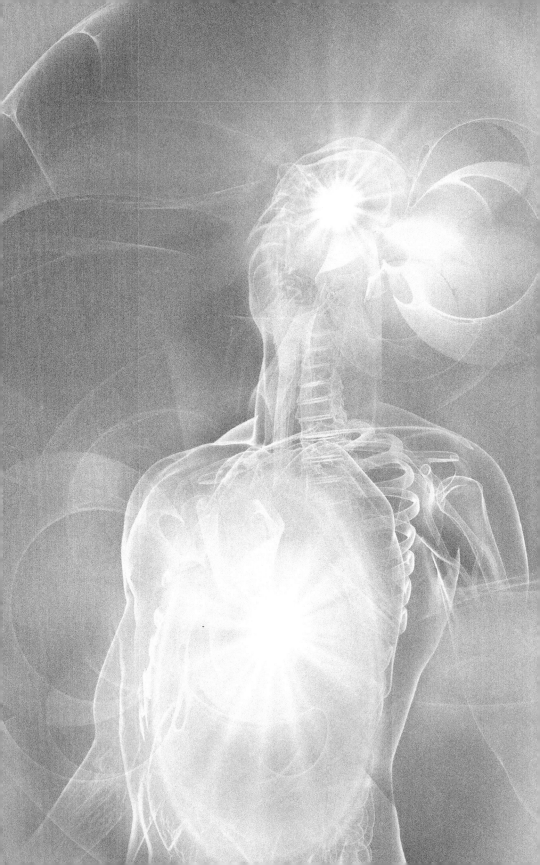

CONTENT

INTRODUCTION

Knowing our spirit, in all its forms and functions, is the key element that allows us to grow as sons of God.

The knowledge of how our inner being was designed has been a hidden mystery for centuries. After much searching, I have come to the conclusion that nothing has been written to shed light with respect to this topic. I was only able to find antique writings by Dr. Watchman Nee, a pioneer in his time, who only superficially covered the true reality and configuration of our spirit. Dr. Paul Trulin also touched on this theme, but neither one had what I longed for.

I wanted to know our inner anatomy, the spirit and soul, with the same passion a medical doctor longs to know the human body.

Scripture says:

> *"But God has revealed them to us through His Spirit. For the Spirit searches all things, yes, the deep things of God. For what man knows the things of a man except the spirit of the man which is in him? Even so no one knows the things of God except the Spirit of God."*
>
> *1 Corinthians 2:10-11*

It was then that I began to seek God deeply, asking Him to show me the spirit of man. After much fasting, much prayer, and hours and days of meditating on this, the Lord visited me and revealed before my eyes, our entire internal configuration. These were days of ever increasing revelation and it filled me with light and understanding.

This book is the result of those visitations which opened up the Scripture to me in an extraordinary way. This is the revelation He gave me in His infinite grace, to make known to those who thirst to know their own spirit. To the Eternal Father be all the glory, for the majestic work He did in every single one of us, giving us the privilege of being made in His image and likeness.

PART I

HOW WE WERE
CREATED

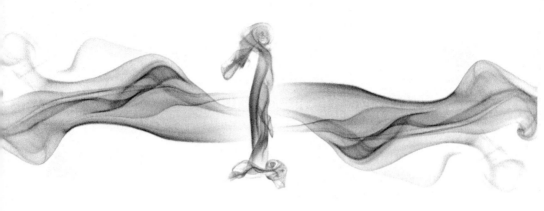

Chapter 1

WE ARE SPIRIT

1. Who are we?

Who are we, really? That is the philosophical question that has motivated the minds and scrutiny of the most distinguished thinkers of all times.

If I were to ask you who you are, at first glance it would seem like an easy question for you to answer. You may respond with, "I am John Smith." Then I would say, "Yes, that is your name, but who are you?"

Then you would think twice, and say, "I am an engineer and I work as a manager at a large firm." Then I would say to you, "Yes, that is your profession, but who are you?"

And that is where the true conflict begins to take place on the inside. Who really is this being, covered by those things we think we are?

In order to understand this, which is not easy to figure out, we must turn our eyes to the origin of man, back to the original design created by our Maker.

Our being is defined by the source of its origin. A baby lion is defined as such because he comes from his father and mother, whom are both lions.

In the same way, the great "I Am," our God the creator, determined that from Him would come forth a creation composed of His substance and nature.

This being would have within himself the ability, authority, intelligence, wisdom, creativity, power and all of the attributes of the Father inherent to His divine genetics.

A. The Origin of Man

Then God said, "Let Us make man in Our image, according to Our likeness; let them have dominion over the fish of the sea, over the birds of the air, and over the cattle, over all the earth and over every creeping thing that creeps on the earth."

So God created man in His own image; in the image of God He created him; male and female He created them.

Genesis 1:26-27

B. In God's Image

God created man in His image. This means that whoever looked upon man, would recognize God in him. As Jesus, the "Last Adam," would say to His disciple Phillip, "He who has seen Me has seen the Father."

Jesus came to restore what had been lost as the result of the fall. In His work and in His own being, Jesus reflects the identity and attributes lost by the first Adam.

It is in the understanding of where we come from and in Whose Image we were created, that we will find the answer to our true identity.

That image is what answers the question of who we truly are; that is, "Sons of God."

God made a family for Himself according to Who He is, in order to give His children dominion and authority over all things. Our spirit is that divine substance from which we were formed.

In essence, that is who we are: Spirits that come from God.

*Furthermore, we have had human fathers who corrected us, and we paid them respect. Shall we not much more readily be in subjection to the **Father of spirits** and live?*

Hebrews 12:9

In the natural, only a father can impart identity in his children. Growing alongside a true father allows us to have a firm and secure identity to go through life. When a father is loving, cares about his child, corrects, affirms and teaches him, the child develops a stable personality.

That person will feel secure and proud to be the child of that father. The maternal figure, regardless of how loving and devoted she is, or how much she gives her children, she will never be able to impart on them their identity.

We take our last name from our father and that determines our genealogy and origin; which is part of our identity, or what identifies us to what family we belong.

However, our basic nature is not the natural one, but the spiritual one. Before we were humans, we were spirits known and named by God.

> *Before I formed you in the womb I **knew you**; before you were born I sanctified you; I ordained you a prophet to the nations.*
>
> *Jeremiah 1:5*

> *Just as He chose us in Him **before the** foundation of the world, that we should be holy and without blame before **Him** in love.*
>
> *Ephesians 1:4*

> *But now, thus says the Lord, who created you, O Jacob, and He who formed you, O Israel: "Fear not, for I have redeemed you; I have called you **by your name**; you are Mine.*
>
> *Isaiah 43:1*

He is the Father of all spirits, and this is the true and eternal nature, which gives us the identity and the understanding of our origin.

God created man just as He is, with a divine ability to know all things. Nowadays, scientists confirm that man only utilizes 2% of his mental ability. A gifted person, such as Albert Einstein, utilizes approximately 10%.

However, this is not the design of God for His most sublime creation. The spirit and soul of Adam were cloaked with all intelligence, wisdom, knowledge and power to govern all creation. He was created to understand and move in two dimensions simultaneously; the natural and the spiritual. Adam could perceive the natural world through his physical senses, but at the same time he had his spiritual senses totally activated and could see the spiritual reality in all its dimensions. At the same time, he could see the trees in paradise that God provided for him to eat from, as well as the spiritual trees. These spiritual trees were the Tree of the knowledge of good and evil and the Tree of Life.

He would speak with the Father in the cool of the day, and also with the animals,. His spirit and his perception had the ability to discern the meaning and intentions of every sound emitted from creation and know what each species was saying.

God had given him dominion and authority over them, and as a result, he could communicate with them. This was made clear when the serpent spoke, and they were not surprised. It was normal for them.

When Adam named the animals, he did not do it randomly. The name had to do with the nature and attributes of every created being. So Adam saw the characteristics that defined each species of animal and gave it the appropriate name. He even knew how they thought. He named the serpent, "astute" which means to have mental ability.

All of this was possible because his earthly nature was covered with the glory of his own spirit, which was in itself a deposit of the very life of God. As a matter of fact, Adam and his wife were also covered with Christ. He is the first light, and all things were made by Him and all things in Him consist. In Him are all the treasures of wisdom and knowledge contained.

*… That their hearts may be encouraged, being knit together in love, and attaining to all riches of the full assurance of understanding, to the **knowledge of the mystery of God, both of the Father and of Christ, in whom are hidden all the treasures of wisdom and knowledge.***

Colossians 2:2-3

Adam's thoughts were continuously illuminated by the manifold wisdom of God. He simply knew all things. He was made full of creativity, art and inventiveness. His spirit had the ability to search out the most complex universes of the microcosm and macrocosm. He understood the most elaborate formulas in mathematics and physics, as well as the perfect harmony of the ecosystem orchestrated by God and each one of its components.

He was full of joy because his spirit breathed the continuous love of His Father, which filled him with plenitude. He was the king of all things and creation would serve him for whatever purpose came from his heart. He was created to be the architect of what would have been cities full of the glory of God. To sum it all up, he was a true son of God.

God's idea was to create a world full of His sons, where He would be the Father and God of us all. Unfortunately, this entire plan was brought down because of the fall.

C. Behind the Scenes

While this entire marvelous scenery was glimmering in harmony and glory, a plan for its destruction was being forged behind the scenes.

Lucifer, the Archangel of wisdom had filled himself with evil and had fallen from heaven along with a third of the angels. These angels, however, were not created in the image and likeness of God and as such, were not redeemable, or the Most High determined that it would be that way.

Lucifer, stripped of his light, his glory and his rank, was sentenced to eternal darkness. From that place, he would look on with horror at the creation of a new lineage of divine beings to which the Father would give His authority.

As a spiritual being, satan did not have access to the natural realm to rule over it as he intended. The serpent in itself was only an animal, limited and incapable of reigning and taking dominion. satan needed someone who had a mind and more elaborate intelligence. He needed a vessel designed to contain a highly complex spirit, and this was the human being.

2. Man is an Incarnate Spirit

We must understand that unlike angels and demons, man is the only spirit created with the ability to operate in two dimensions at the same time because man is a spirit who dwells in a fleshly body.

For the spiritual and the earthly to work together, it is necessary to have a third element that will allow them to communicate and make them compatible with each other.

For this purpose, God created a magnificent device called the "soul."

And the Lord God formed man of the dust of the ground, and breathed into his nostrils the breath of life; and man became a living being.

Genesis 2:7

As God blew His breath in this body made of clay, He formed not only the human spirit, but also this third element within him.

In other words, we were created spirits, which live in a body and have a soul to understand and process both the spiritual and the natural worlds. We are the only creation with this tripartite composition.

In a moment we will see why this device was so coveted by the devil.

The soul is made from the same ethereal substance as the spirit. Psychology, oblivious to the life of the spirit, only considers man as body and soul, but the Bible mentions all three parts:

Now may the God of peace Himself sanctify you completely; and may your whole spirit, soul, and body be preserved blameless at the coming of our Lord Jesus Christ.

1 Thessalonians 5: 23

When we imagine our soul and spirit, we think of it in the form of a ghost; a humanoid figure similar to us, made from a volatile substance, invisible to the natural eye.

Others, more advanced, such as Dr. Watchman Nee in the beginning of the 20th Century, saw the spirit as a composition made up of communion, intuition, and conscience. He also saw the soul as a combination of the mind, emotions and will. This revelation was relevant and undoubtedly a foundation for all of us, but it doesn't stop there. It has been growing and God is bringing new light so we may analyze it.

We all agree that defining the body as simply a mass made up of a head, trunk and extremities would fall extremely short of what this marvelous machine is, called the human body.

Our organism is composed of eight systems with multiple organs all interconnected. These are the cardiovascular system, respiratory system, digestive system, nervous system, skeletal system, muscular system, reproductive system and immune system. Also at microscopic levels, there is a great quantity of things occurring within the chemistry of the brain and the cells. The human body is so complex, and is created in such a supernatural form that modern science has yet to discover all of its components.

In this same way, our spirit and soul are composed of a series of systems and organs, which allow them to discern and know both the spiritual and natural worlds.

As I mentioned earlier, the spirit of man does not have access to the natural world except through the soul.

Let me give you a clear example. I am going to compare our spirit with a movie recorded on a DVD. If I do not have a DVD player, I will never be able to watch that movie. The DVD player has a decoder that translates what was recorded onto the surface of the DVD disc so the images can be seen on my television set, allowing me to watch the movie.

The soul is the DVD player made from a spiritual substance, which decodes the things of the spirit as well as the dimensions of the invisible kingdom, and makes them visible, audible and understandable.

The soul is what makes a human being different from any other spirit, either angelic or demonic.

It is the perfect machine, joined to the spirit, which gives man the ability to govern and interpret spiritual dynamics from God or the devil.

The soul of man corresponds to everything the spirit of man is. It is like a mirror that reflects everything that is the spirit so it can be decoded. Once the soul interprets what comes from the spirit, it transfers it to the body, because the three parts are intrinsically linked together.

The body will then receive either the benefits that come from the Spirit of God or the consequences that come from the spirit that is still contaminated.

The soul, having the same components as the spirit, can survive on its own and be independent from the spirit.

Now then, God created the soul of man, so that man could interpret nothing less than the Spirit of God, which lived in Adam. That is what made this extraordinary, never before created, machine so desirable to satan.

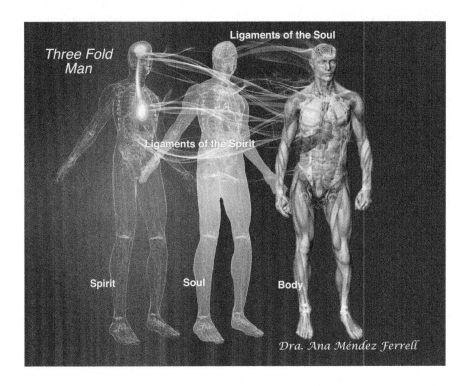

Figure 1 - Tripartite Man

Now since this machine had the ability to interpret, reveal and manifest everything God was, it also had the ability to interpret any kind of spirits from darkness. It was an instrument designed by the Creator to govern the Earth.

satan knew that among all the animals he would not find a host where he could place a spirit of humanism, witchcraft, drug addiction or any other spirit. Only the magnificent soul of man could contain them and reveal their thoughts and conduct.

3. Identity loses the Source of its Origin

satan, seeing the greatness and perfection of the soul, coveted it for himself. This was the instrument that, once under his control, would give him access to the government of the earth and the destruction of his new adversaries, the Sons of God. So He came up with a plan, and possessed the astute serpent to deceive man and his wife.

Now, the big obstacle was man's free will, one of the complex organs of the soul. If the devil could sow doubt in the heart of one of them regarding the word God had given them, and chose to believe him instead, he would obtain his objective.

God had said:

> *... but of the tree of the knowledge of good and evil you shall not eat, for in the day that you eat of it you shall surely die.*
>
> *Genesis 2:17*

> *Then the serpent said to the woman, "You will not surely die. For God knows that in the day you eat of it your eyes will be opened and you will be like God, knowing good and evil."*
>
> *Genesis 3:4-5*

Eating from the Tree of life was the divine provision given so that man could live eternally in Paradise. Eating from the tree of the knowledge of good and evil was the alternative; and the trigger from the kingdom of darkness, which would separate man from his Father and his God. The consequence of eating from this tree is the separation of the dimensions of the Spirit, from the dimensions of the Earth, and it continues to do so in those who still eat from it.

When Adam and his wife took this step and decided to eat from the alternative tree, they died to their communion with God. Their spirit fell into a state of sleep and their soul, which had been covered by the splendor of their spirit, was left naked and condemned to death. It is the condition of the spirit, whether it is alive or dead (state of sleep), which determines the final destiny of the soul.

After the fall, the spirit lost its dominion and power and its ability to rule. The soul had become now the king and lord of man, governed by the knowledge and wisdom of darkness. In that moment the "ego" or the "self" rose up within man, which would oppose the spirit, just as the two trees oppose each other.

Jesus Christ is the Tree of life, who is the light of eternal knowledge. He is the first light that illuminates the understanding of the spirit to know God and His unfathomable mysteries. He is the very life of the spirit that awakens the whole being, spirit, soul and body in order to fill it with His eternal essence.

A man that has been conceived from the life of the Spirit of God, by Jesus Christ, knows he is a Son of God, and receives his identity from Him.

A soul stripped from God is under the light of science and earthly knowledge. The same is true for a religious or carnal man who is in darkness and feels the emptiness within, as a result of his dormant spirit. He feels like an orphan, and his identity depends on the value others give him, or from his own fantasy world.

The "ego" became a god, just as the serpent had said to the woman. However, one that does not know how to be a god, has neither the answers nor the power he should have as such. It lives from the lies of a title that exalts it and feeds it; terrified of having to confront its own deception, and seeing its house of cards tumble down.

Chapter 2

ENCOUNTERING OUR SPIRIT
ONCE AGAIN

1. First and Second Adam

Man lost his original state as well as his ability to reunite with his Creator. No matter how much the fallen soul longed to, it could not reunite with God, because they were now of two different natures, and therefore incompatible. God is light and holiness, and man is darkness and sin.

Only God as creator could repair what had been broken, and bring to life what was now dead. God had to create a way for the soul of man to be once again formed into its original design. This way it could be reconnected to the spirit of man, and have the ability to receive the flow of eternal and divine life.

This is what Jesus came to do in the world; restore what had been lost. He had to become flesh and soul in order to destroy the kingdom of darkness, sin, sickness and death as a man.

Having done so, He sat on the throne of glory in the heavens as the "Second Adam" reuniting human nature with the divine.

He had to retake the position of government and dominion over all the earth, but this time, holding the title of King of Kings and Lord of Lords.

Therefore, just as through one man sin entered the world, and death through sin, and thus death spread to all men, because all sinned.

Romans 5:12

For since by man came death, by Man also came the resurrection of the dead. For as in Adam all die, even so in Christ all shall be made alive.

1 Corinthians 15:21-22

And so it is written, "The first man Adam became a living being." The last Adam became a life-giving spirit.

1 Corinthians 15:45

2. The Kingdom of God is Spiritual

The first Adam lost his access to the Kingdom of God, which is a spiritual dimension. Jesus, the second Adam, came to bring His Father's Kingdom so that man, united with His spirit, could once again enjoy it.

Among the many truths that Jesus came to establish, there are four that I believe are fundamental in regard to this topic.

A. Heaven and Earth came back together in Jesus

which He made to abound toward us in all wisdom and prudence, having made known to us the mystery of His will, according to His good pleasure which He purposed in Himself, that in the dispensation of the fullness of the times He might gather together in one all things in Christ, both which are in heaven and which are on earth - in Him.

Ephesians 1:8-10

As we have just read, it was Jesus' will to bring back together all things; those who are in heaven as well as those who are on earth. This took place when Jesus died on the cross and resurrected, having fulfilled everything that had been written[1].

This means there was no longer a division between the two dimensions. **In Jesus**, man is once again in the same condition as the first Adam, having access to everything that is in heaven and on earth.

The key here is to understand what it means to be, **In Jesus**, since this is a spiritual position in which someone has been covered, submerged and filled with the Spirit of Christ[2].

---

[1] Several scriptures speak of the fulfillment of the ages. These are some of the scriptures:He then would have had to suffer often since the foundation of the world; but now, once at the end of the ages, He has appeared to put away sin by the sacrifice of Himself. (Hebrews 9:26)

Then He said to them, "These are the words which I spoke to you while I was still with you, that all things must be fulfilled which were written in the Law of Moses and the Prophets and the Psalms concerning Me." (Luke 24:44)

[2] I recommend you read the Book "Immersed in Him", written by my husband, L. Emerson Ferrell, so that you may understand the meaning of these powerful words.

As Paul the apostle said:

> *for in Him we live and move and have our being, as also some of your own poets have said, 'For we are also His offspring.'*
>
> *Acts 17:28*

What Jesus did was to bring the spiritual reality of heaven, and made it accessible to us again.

> *Let us therefore come boldly to the throne of grace, that we may obtain mercy, and find grace to help in time of need.*
>
> *Hebrews 4:16*

The throne of His Grace does not simply refer to receiving grace from Him, as merely a way of speaking, but it refers to entering into a real dimension and receiving from Him.

To think that we have the ability to enter the heavenly dimensions is inconceivable to the natural mind because the fallen soul cannot perceive such greatness, but the redeemed spirit can.

> *But the natural man does not receive the things of the Spirit of God, for they are foolishness to him; nor can he know them, because they are spiritually discerned.*
>
> *1 Corinthians 2:14*

In order to understand this, we must look at the second truth, which I want to emphasize.

B. We Must be born of the Water and of the Spirit

Being Born Again has become a cliché and a common phrase in Christian vocabulary. Unfortunately, in most cases, the depth of this vital truth, has been lost.

The spirit is in a state of death or sleep because of sin and is awakened and engendered when we come to Christ.

But as many as received Him, to them He gave the right to become children of God, to those who believe in His name: who were (engendered), not of blood, nor of the will of the flesh, nor of the will of man, but of God.

John 1:12-13

There is a difference between being *engendered* and being born.

It is like when a child is conceived in the womb. The child is already alive and exists, but has not been born into this world. The child must be submerged in amniotic fluid for nine months, before he is born. During this time, the fetus is being nourished by the waters he is immersed in. He is in the process of being formed, so that at the given time, the baby can function, see, hear, feel and move in the new world he is about to be born into.

The same thing happens to our spirit. We are engendered by the divine seed, which is Jesus. Then it is our responsibility to remain in the waters of the Spirit of God, which is achieved through:

- Worship and intimacy with the Father, Son and
  Holy Spirit, who give us the living waters to drink.

but whoever drinks of the water that I shall give him will never thirst. But the water that I shall give him will become in him a fountain of water springing up into everlasting life.

John 4:14

God is Spirit, and those who worship Him must worship in spirit and truth.

John 4:24

- Through sanctification and washing, through
  the study and meditation of the Word of God.

*Husbands, love your wives, just as Christ also loved the church and gave Himself for her, that He might sanctify and cleanse her with the **washing** of water by the word,*

Ephesians 5:25-26

C. Those Born of the Spirit have entered the Dimension of Heaven

When Jesus introduced the theme of a new birth in the Spirit, He was referring to entering the heavenly realm.

Being "Born of God" is not being a church member or reading scripture. Jesus clearly taught us what those "Born of God" are like, and stated their characteristics.

They have the ability to see the Kingdom of God because they have entered in, and they have become like the wind, not knowing where it comes from or where it is headed.

Let us consider this concept from a deeper angle in order to grab hold of the heavenly truths that Jesus wanted to relay to Nicodemus.

> *Jesus answered and said to him, "Most assuredly, I say to you, unless one is born again,* **he cannot see the kingdom of God.***"*
>
> *John 3:3*

> *Jesus answered, "Most assuredly, I say to you, unless one is born of water and the Spirit,* **he cannot enter the kingdom of God.**
>
> *That which is born of the flesh is flesh, and that which is born of the Spirit is spirit.*
>
> *Do not marvel that I said to you, 'You must be born again.' The wind blows where it wishes, and you hear the sound of it, but cannot tell where it comes from and where it goes. So is everyone who is born of the Spirit."*
>
> *John 3:5-8*

Our spirit, which had been asleep, received the life of Jesus after we repented of our vain lifestyle and we knowingly invoked His name. Now our spirit must be formed, and the areas we have never used or even knew existed must be awakened.

That is why it is so important to know our spirit and understand how it works, so we will know which parts must still be developed.

Jesus, the Son of God, lived as a true "Born Again"-being here on earth, knowing and moving in both dimensions at the same time. When He told Nicodemus that those who are born of God are like the wind, He is referring to the "Ruah"[3], the Spirit of God within the spirit of man.

Wind is the only element that moves independently from the earth, because it is not from the earth; it is from the Spirit. All of the other elements such as earth, fire and water are connected to physical matter, but the wind is not.

Wind comes from a heavenly place. Scientists are able to measure its intensity and direction, but do not know what it is or where it comes from.

*He causes the vapors to ascend from the ends of the earth;
He makes lightning for the rain; He brings the wind out
of His treasuries.*

Psalms 135:7

Those born of the Spirit have been formed inside of God and He blows them and leads them as He wills. They are in heaven and on earth at the same time, and that is why they can "See" the Kingdom and move in it.

*If I have told you earthly things and you do not believe,
how will you believe if I tell you heavenly things? No one
has ascended to heaven but He who came down from
heaven, that is, the Son of Man **who is in heaven**.*

John 3:12-13

---

[3]   Ruah, Hebrew word which means wind.

Notice that Jesus said this before His death and ascension into heaven. He is telling Nicodemus that being born of the Spirit gives man access to heaven and it is possible to be in heaven and on earth at the same time.

Every awakened and vivified spirit understands this. If the spirit is being formed and is growing on the inside, it will long for the moment of its birth more than anything else. However, a slumbering spirit will see this as something humanly impossible.

The reality of the Kingdom of God is visible, audible and palpable for those who are born of God. The seed of the Almighty has been formed inside them and is manifested in their way of being and acting.

> *Whoever has been born of God does not sin, for His seed remains in him; and he cannot sin, because he has been born of God.*
>
> *In this the children of God and the children of the devil are manifest: Whoever does not practice righteousness is not of God, nor is he who does not love his brother.*
>
> 1 John 3: 9-10

This is the true condition of a spirit that has been awakened and quickened by God and has been born into the Kingdom of God.

D. The Kingdom of God is invisible and can only be discerned spiritually

The Kingdom of God is a kingdom of the Spirit.

This dimension is different from that of the earth. Its wisdom and ways are higher than those of the material world. Therefore, only an awakened spirit can enter it and understand it.

> *However, we speak wisdom among those who are mature, yet not the wisdom of this age, nor of the rulers of this age, who are coming to nothing.*
>
> *But we speak the wisdom of God in a mystery, the hidden wisdom which God ordained before the ages for our glory, which none of the rulers of this age knew; for had they known, they would not have crucified the Lord of glory.*
>
> *1 Corinthians 2:6-8*

The world and its way of analyzing things, its wisdom and its goals are very different from God's.

Israel's princes, its priests, scribes and doctors of the law in the time of Jesus did not know the things of the spirit. Their wisdom and understanding had a carnal logic, because their spirits were asleep in the same manner as the first Adam. So when Jesus told them that His Kingdom would not come visibly and would not be located in a particular place on earth, including Jerusalem, they were offended and disqualified Him as a potential Messiah.

> *Now when He was asked by the Pharisees when the kingdom of God would come, He answered them and said, "The kingdom of God does not come with observation; nor will they say, 'See here!' or 'See there!' For indeed, the kingdom of God is within you."*
>
> *Luke 17:20*

The wisdom of God, by the Spirit, is the one from heaven, because it is the unlimited Mind of Christ. God designed for us to know His mysteries and His inscrutable thoughts, so we could be covered with His Glory.

But as it is written: "Eye has not seen, nor ear heard,

Nor have entered into the heart of man

The things which God has prepared for those who love Him."

*But God has revealed them to us **through His Spirit**. **For the Spirit searches all things, yes, the deep things of God.***

1 Corinthians 2:9-10

The awakened spirit of a Son of God is by nature a researcher. It is not passive and is not waiting for others to provide answers. He knows that he can know all things in God, and does not stop until all his questions are answered.

One of these great questions is the central concept of our study, "What is the spirit of man like, and how does it operate?"

For what man knows the things of a man except the spirit of the man which is in him? Even so no one knows the things of God except the Spirit of God.

1 Corinthians 2:11

Our spirit is the one that knows everything concerning who we are as Sons of God. It knows the identity of who we truly are as men made in the image of God.

Our soul does not know the things of man. Our carnal mind does not have this knowledge nor can understand or decipher it.

Psychology and psychiatry with all its great doctors cannot understand who man truly is or how he functions. Many of them believe we come from a monkey. That is why, when they come across a complex mental disorder, they solve it by filling up the patient with medication.

How could Nicodemus understand that Jesus was in Heaven and on Earth at the same time or that someone could be like the wind?

Jesus spoke in the language and wisdom of the Spirit because His words were Spirit and they were life.

> *It is the Spirit who gives life; the flesh profits nothing.*
> *The words that I speak to you are spirit, and they are life.*
> *It is the Spirit who gives life; the flesh profits nothing.*
> *The words that I speak to you are spirit, and they are life.*
>
> *John 6:63*

He came to His own, yet His own did not receive Him because they loved their souls in darkness, along with their logic and doctrines, more than the light of the Spirit of Life. The words of Jesus however, remained on the earth eternally, so that His Spirit would vivify anyone who receives them.

It is in our spirit where we understand everything that has been given to us by God. We do not live waiting for the moment of our death to understand how we were made, instead, He manifests and reveals this to us.

*Now we have received, not the spirit of the world, but the Spirit who is from God, that we might know the things that have been freely given to us by God. These things we also speak, **not in words which man's wisdom teaches but which the Holy Spirit teaches**, comparing spiritual things with spiritual.*

1 Corinthians 2:12-13

The spirit has a very special way of expressing itself. It uses different words given by the Spirit; because the Spiritual reality has different physics, and dynamics that does not exist in the material world.

That is why the carnal or soul driven man cannot understand what we are discussing; to him it sounds like something out of this world.

Then he refers to it as "being crazy", "not possible", "it sounds like new age" or "that is fantasy." They even blaspheme against the Holy Spirit criticizing what they do not understand.

But the natural, nonspiritual man does not accept or welcome or admit into his heart the gifts and teachings and revelations of the Spirit of God, for they are folly (meaningless nonsense) to him; and he is incapable of knowing them (of progressively recognizing, understanding, and becoming better acquainted with them) because they are spiritually discerned and estimated and appreciated.

But the spiritual man tries all things (he examines, investigates, inquiries into, questions, and discerns all things), yet is himself to be put on trial and judged by no one [he can read the meaning of everything, but no one can properly discern or appraise or get an insight into him].

1 Corinthians 2:14-15 AMP

For "who has known the mind of the Lord that he may instruct Him?" But we have the mind of Christ.

1 Corinthians 2:16

The natural mind cannot understand God's thoughts nor can it discern the believer who has reached a level of maturity as the result of having been born of the Spirit of God.

This spiritual stature is the fruit of our spirit being fused with God's spirit, and in this manner, He places in us the mind of Christ.

.

PART II

THE ANATOMY
OF THE SPIRIT

Chapter 3

THE VISION OF OUR SPIRIT

When I realized the only way I would truly know who I am was through knowing my spirit, it was troubling to know how little we, as Sons of God, understood this particular topic. I then began to seek books and documents that would shed light on where I could start.

The only thing I was able to find was the trilogy, "The Spiritual Man" by Dr. Watchman Nee which He wrote at the end of the 19th Century. I also found "My Body, His Life" by Dr. Paul Trulin, written in the 1980's.

They both spoke of various functions of the spirit or of the fruit or gifts of the spirit, but neither described our spirit. What was it like? What was its shape or anatomy? How does it work? How could we connect with it to discover it and use it to its fullest capacity?

The most I found in these two books were some illustrations which identified three simple components: communion, intuition and conscience. However, to me, this was like thinking that my body was composed of only three large masses called head, torso and extremities.

Something on the inside told me that just like our physical body is composed of systems and organs, majestically orchestrated within, the soul and spirit were similarly complex.

I knew we had spiritual eyes and ears to see and hear God. I also heard there was a warehouse full of organs in heaven, and that angels descended and gave them to those whose body parts were atrophied. I witnessed many miracles that occurred in this manner. Those organs and body parts that came from the invisible realm were obviously spiritual in origin. They were spiritual first, and then manifested in the flesh.

This, along with many other experiences in the Spirit, led me to search the mind of Christ and ask Him to show me the spirit of man.

I wanted to know what we were like. I had the same curiosity a medical student has to discover how the human body functions, to discover our inner being.

One night, after much fasting and inquiring God, the Father visited me and I saw in front of me the spirit of man.

I was captivated, and marveled when I saw how we were made in the image and likeness of God. Obviously, I was seeing something that my mind could not conceive in human words. I was in awe watching, but could not grasp the fullness of that impressive configuration. This was only the beginning of a gold mine of heavenly knowledge that was opened before my eyes.

It was the true manifestation of the word:

"Eye has not seen, nor ear heard, nor have entered in the heart of man."

1 Corinthians 2:9

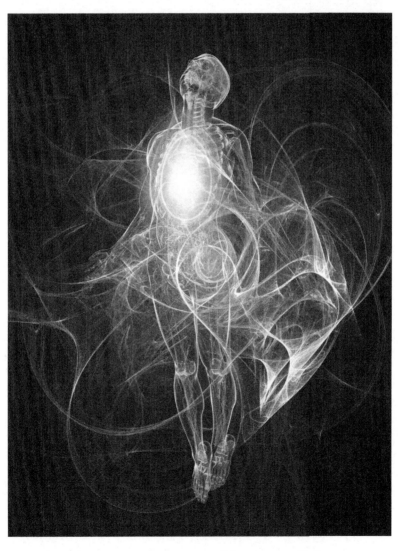

Figure 2 - First Vision of the Spirit of Man

Attempting to draw it was a very complicated task because it consisted of many intertwined systems which were unveiled and manifested before my eyes, one by one. I decided to try and draw them one by one and break it down in this manner.

The teaching began after the first vision, and God gave me this mysterious scripture in the Bible (I placed the interpretation of the phrases in parenthesis "( )" to aid in its comprehension):

In the day when the keepers of the house tremble, (the hands and arms of the elderly) and the strong men bow down; when the (chewing of the) grinders cease because they are few, and those that look through the windows (eyes) grow dim; (eye sight)

when the doors (lips) are shut in the streets, and the sound of grinding is low; (can no longer chew) When one rises up at the sound of a bird, (faint sound of the song), and all the daughters of music (the voice and hearing) are brought low.

also they are afraid of height, and of terrors in the way; when the almond tree blossoms, (white hair) the grasshopper (the lightest) is a burden, and desire fails. For man goes to his eternal home, and the mourners go about the streets.

Remember your Creator before the silver cord is loosed, or the golden bowl is broken, or the pitcher shattered at the fountain, or the wheel broken at the well.

Then the dust will return to the earth as it was, and the spirit will return to God who gave it.

Ecclesiastes 12:3-7 (with Author's interpretation)

In the passage of scripture between Verses 3 and 5, King Solomon describes the moment when man is about to go to his eternal dwelling. We see the entire poetic description of the wearing away of the body in old age.

Then in Verse 6, there is a description of the moment when the spirit and soul leave the body. This is where King Solomon describes the configuration of the spirit of man.

Chapter 4

THE SILVER CORD

As stated previously, humans are the only spirits that were created to have a physical body. Now, the spirit and soul are composed of a spiritual substance and the body is composed of a physical substance. Given that they differ in substance, an element is needed in order to keep them united. This is the function of the silver cord. When it breaks, man dies.

The new age movement has usurped a great deal of Biblical principles and has corrupted them. These principles are only valid in the context that God spoke them; when not used in that way, they are defiled.

The spirit of man has the ability to leave the physical body to enter into the spirit realm. God gave man this ability; he was created that way. This was not invented by the devil; it is God's design.

The Spirit of God has taken and continues to take several prophets to spiritual places, and their bodies remain alive in the earthly realm. Such was the case with Ezekiel, who was taken in the Spirit to see what was happening in the temple in Jerusalem.

> *He stretched out the form of a hand, and took me by a lock of my hair; and the Spirit lifted me up between earth and heaven, and brought me in visions of God to Jerusalem, to the door of the north gate of the inner court, where the seat of the image of jealousy was, which provokes to jealousy.*
>
> *Ezekiel 8:3*

The expression "took me by a lock of my hair" refers to the top part of Ezekiel's head. That is where he felt his spirit being lifted up between heaven and earth.

In other occasions, he was taken to the heavenly city.

> *In the visions of God He took me into the land of Israel and set me on a very high mountain; on it toward the south was something like the structure of a city.*
>
> *...*
>
> *And the man said to me, "Son of man, look with your eyes and hear with your ears, and fix your mind on everything I show you; for **you were brought here** so that I might show them to you. Declare to the house of Israel everything you see.*
>
> *Ezekiel 40:2; 4*

Here, he refers to this experience as "visions of God," however, the angel tells him he was actually taken there.

We see similar experiences in the New Testament, when Paul the Apostle is taken to the third heaven and he does not know if it took place in the body or outside the body.

I know a man in Christ who fourteen years ago — whether in the body I do not know, or whether out of the body I do not know, God knows — such a one was caught up to the third heaven.

And I know such a man — whether in the body or out of the body I do not know, God knows —

how he was caught up into Paradise and heard inexpressible words, which it is not lawful for a man to utter.

2 Corinthians 12:2-4

We also see John the Apostle, throughout the book of Revelation being taken from one place to another in the spiritual realm.

These experiences are biblical and part of our spiritual abilities.

We must remember that the devil is an imitator and not a creator. He knows the spiritual world and the abilities of the spirit. For centuries, he has revealed himself to his followers and they have twisted everything with the help of demons. They have been able to do many things with great power, at the astonishment of everyone. However, God's design is not for them to have extraordinary powers, but for us to have them in Christ. This way we could establish God's kingdom on Earth and undo the works of the devil.

That is why the Holy Spirit wants to give us the wisdom of God, which neither the princes of this world, warlocks nor witches can ever know.

Further ahead, when I will speak about the functions of the spirit, I will describe this in more detail. In the meantime, we will continue to describe the anatomy and parts of the spirit.

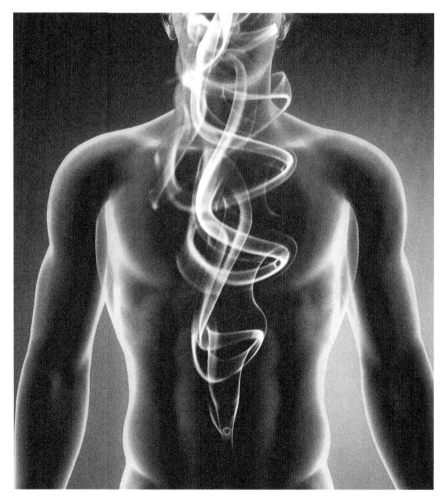

Figure 3 - The Silver Cord

Figure 4 - Man entering the Spiritual Dimension

It is important to point out that entering the spiritual dimensions is very different than astral projection. I will explain the spiritual doors they use, later on.

In a Godly experience the first thing we need to understand is that God initiates it, not man. John, the Apostle, while at the Island of Patmos, said he was in the Spirit. Once he was in that state, he was able to experience Jesus in His Glory (Revelation 1).

However, God wanted to take him to higher places and it was God that told John to "come up higher." In that moment, he entered a different dimension where he was able to see all the heavenly activity around the throne of God (Revelation 4).

Therefore, entering the spiritual dimension, or being in the spirit, is an ability we can all have, but being translated to higher dimensions, to other places or traveling through time is something that must be initiated by God, and not by ourselves.

Whatever the experience is, when it is from God, the person never loses his/her conscience state. The person is able to communicate with others around him and narrate what he is seeing. The experience can end at whatever moment the person wants.

That was the case of John the Apostle I just described. He was in all those spiritual places that we read about in Revelation but he was describing them to his disciple, Prochorus, who wrote the book by hand[4].

When an experience is not from God, it is known as an astral projection. The person is taken out of the body by a guardian spirit which will maintain the connection between the person's body and spirit. The person will lose consciousness and will be in a trance, unable to speak with anyone. The experience will not end when the person decides it should end, but when the demonic spirit returns him to his body.

---

[4] The historical information regarding how the Book of Revelation was documented is found in the book, "An Island Called Patmos" written by William Edgar Geil. Harvard University 1896

Chapter 5

THE GOLDEN BOWL

We will now continue with the following element as described by King Solomon in a passage of Scripture we shall study.

> *Remember your Creator before the silver cord is loosed, or the **golden bowl** is broken, or the pitcher is shattered at the fountain, or the wheel is broken at the well.*
>
> *Ecclesiastes 12:6*

The golden bowl is the container where the seed of life enters in order to awaken our spirit. It is the place life flows out of. It is our being's Holy of Holies.

To this day, it has been taught in biblical seminaries, that our tripartite being is similar to Moses' Tabernacle in the Old Testament.

It consisted of three parts: The outer court, the Holy Place and the Holy of Holies.

This made it easy to associate it with the three parts of our being: body, soul and spirit respectively.

The Holy of Holies was the place where the presence of God dwelled, within the "Ark of the Covenant." That is why ancient theologians related this to our spirit.

It was believed that once the Lord entered the heart through the conversion of a believer, the spirit of man was totally sanctified and everything in him was filled with God.

This sounds wonderful, but it is not precisely the reality of what takes place when Christ comes to dwell in His sons, nor is it what the Bible describes.

Our spirit, having been in a dormant state due to sin, was filled with iniquity. This corrupted our inner self, and unless we purge of it out of ourselves, we will continue to have dormant areas in our spirit.

Paul, the Apostle, writes to the Corinthians stating the following:

> *Therefore, having these promises, beloved, let us cleanse ourselves from all filthiness of the flesh **and spirit**, perfecting holiness in the fear of God.*
>
> *2 Corinthians 7:1*

Also, Prophet Malachi speaks of infidelity as a sin that affects the spirit directly.

"For the Lord God of Israel says that He hates divorce,

For it covers one's garment with violence," Says the Lord of hosts.

"Therefore take heed to your spirit that you do not deal treacherously"

Malachi 2:16

These scriptures, especially the first one, which was spoken to the saints in Corinth, shows that even though Christ lived in their hearts, they still had to clean their spirits.

If I try to understand this according to the analogy of the Tabernacle, I will find myself in the conflicting argument that Christ cannot dwell where there is corruption and iniquity.

If on the contrary, we understand the anatomy of the spirit, we will see that Christ comes to dwell in a specific place. This is a place reserved for the presence of God in the spirit called the "Golden Bowl."

It is from this place where life flows, and where it is determined whether we belong to either God, or to death and the devil. This area is directly connected to the spiritual heart and soul of man.

Keep your heart with all diligence, for out of it spring the issues of life.

Proverbs 4:23

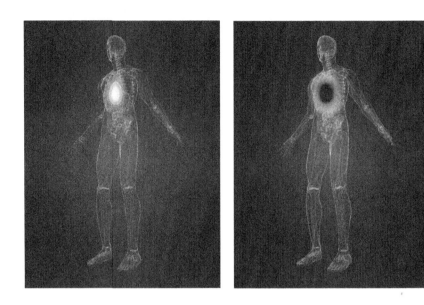

Figure 5/6 - The Golden Bowl / Golden Bowl in a State of Death

When someone is possessed by demons, or is under the power of the devil, it takes place in the "Golden Bowl." Death entered Adam through this place. It is precisely in this place where eternal life or perdition is determined. Anyone who has not filled himself with Jesus has his golden bowl under the power of darkness.

> *He has delivered us from the power of darkness and conveyed us into the kingdom of the Son of His love*
>
> *Colossians 1:13*

The golden bowl is the altar of God, which Ezekiel saw. It is the place in our spirit from where the river of God flows.

Then he brought me back to the door of the temple; and there was water, flowing from under the threshold of the temple toward the east,

Ezekiel 47:1a

The east represents the origin of all things, which is God Himself. When the heart leans toward the Father to be engendered by Him, the seed of life enters the golden bowl and begins to produce the waters of the Spirit.

The waters begin to flow to awaken and fill our entire being; spirit, soul and body with life, so that we may be born into the Kingdom of God and its eternal dimensions. The river is full of life and wherever these waters reach and touch, they begin to awaken and heal our inner being.

And behold, the glory of the God of Israel came from the way of the east. His voice was like the sound of many waters; and the earth shone with His glory.

Ezekiel 43:2

And it shall be that every living thing that moves, wherever the rivers go, will live. There will be a very great multitude of fish, because these waters go there; for they will be healed, and everything will live wherever the river goes.

Ezekiel 47:9

The glory and the fire of the Spirit shine in these waters. They bring healing to the waters of the spirit, which had been asleep, and thus, filled with corruption and iniquity. From there they flow into the soul to form a new complete and beautiful creature that can manifest God. Once the waters have completely filled our inner being, they begin to flow and give life to anyone who drinks from them.

This is the part of the spirit Jesus was referring to when He spoke to the Samaritan woman who was drawing water from Jacob's well.

> *Jesus answered and said to her, "Whoever drinks of this water will thirst again, but whoever drinks of the water that I shall give him will never thirst. But the water that I shall give him will become in him a fountain of water springing up into everlasting life."*
>
> *John 4:13-14*

The water from this bowl comes from God and is the only one that can quench our thirst. We may drink from the waters of great men and women of God, but eventually we will thirst again. It is only when we drink from our own bowl that we are satisfied. The fountain within us connects us with God and produces this living water. This water is filled with true love, revelation, resurrection, knowledge of God, hidden mysteries and everything else our spirit and soul need to be nourished and grow.

This is the place of intimate communion between God and man, where both spirits are fused together to form a new man. It is in this place where our spirit contemplates the glory of God and begins to be formed into His image.

Now the Lord is the Spirit; and where the Spirit of the Lord is, there is liberty. But we all, with unveiled face, beholding as in a mirror the glory of the Lord, are being transformed into the same image from glory to glory, just as by the Spirit of the Lord.

2 Corinthians 3:17-18

It is from this place that Jesus was able to say, "He who has seen Me has seen the Father." That is where the splendor of the glory began to invade His entire being, during the transfiguration.

It is the Ark of the Covenant within us; the true habitation of God within man, the temple of His Glory in us.

It is the place where the marriage between Jesus and His bride takes place. In the same way a man and a woman come together and become one flesh in the marriage bed, the Spirit of God must come together with man's spirit. Then we stop being ourselves, and become one Spirit with God.

But he who is joined to the Lord is one spirit with Him.

1 Corinthians 6:17

Paul the Apostle spoke of this great mystery, comparing a marriage in the natural, to that of Christ and His Church.

So husbands ought to love their own wives as their own bodies; he who loves his wife loves himself.

For no one ever hated his own flesh, but nourishes and cherishes it, just as the Lord does the church.

For we are members of His body, of His flesh and of His bones.

"For this reason a man shall leave his father and mother and be joined to his wife, and the two shall become one flesh."

This is a great mystery, but I speak concerning Christ and the church.

Ephesians 5:28-32

It is made very clear in this scripture that in order to be the body of Christ, members of His body, of His flesh, and of His bones, we must be joined in marriage with Him.

We cannot say we are His body, and yet be waiting for some wedding to take place in the unknown future, as some have stipulated. This is a terrible mistake that robs all power, communion, rights and privileges that the Church has, as the wife of the Lamb.

This marriage union is the central concept and the heart of the Gospel. It is the powerful petition that Jesus prayed to the Father, that we would be one in them in the same manner that they are one.

"I do not pray for these alone, but also for those who will believe in Me through their word;

*that **they all may be one, as You, Father, are in Me, and I in You;** that they also may be one in Us, that the world may believe that You sent Me.*

And the glory which You gave Me I have given them, that they may be one just as We are one:

I in them, and You in Me; that they may be made perfect in one, and that the world may know that You have sent Me, and have loved them as You have loved Me.

John 17:20-23

It is in this bowl where the fusing together of both spirits produces intimacy, or the "knowing God".

And this is eternal life, that they may know You, the only true God, and Jesus Christ whom You have sent.

John 17:3

In Scripture, the word "know" in many cases refers to the act of a man having intimacy with his wife. The following is an example:

Now Adam knew Eve his wife, and she conceived and bore Cain, and said, "I have acquired a man from the Lord."

Genesis 4:1

This same concept applies to intimate union in the spiritual sense, or to "know" God, which is what produces eternal life in us. The latter one does not refer to our immortality, but to the life of the Father, fusing itself with ours, and making us one Spirit with Him.

For as a young man marries a virgin, so shall your sons marry you;

And as the bridegroom rejoices over the bride, so shall your God rejoice over you.

Isaiah 62:5

It is the Spirit of God in us, which produces the water of life that flows from our altar. The water from this fusion is what brings healing, and brings to life everything it touches. It is what engenders the plantings of the Lord, which are the Sons of God.

And it shall be that every living thing that moves, wherever the rivers go, will live. There will be a very great multitude of fish, because these waters go there; for they will be healed, and everything will live wherever the river goes.

Ezekiel 47:9

There are two rivers, God's river and our river, but ultimately it is just one river because He has united with His spouse. Together they produce these trees, that are the planting of the Lord, which will heal the land.

Along the bank of the river, on this side and that, will grow all kinds of trees used for food; their leaves will not wither, and their fruit will not fail. They will bear fruit every month, because their water flows from the sanctuary. Their fruit will be for food, and their leaves for medicine."

Ezekiel 47:12

The Spirit and the bride united can call unto a lost world to come and drink of the waters of God.

And the Spirit and the bride say, "Come!" And let him who hears say, "Come!" And let him who thirsts come. Whoever desires, let him take the water of life freely.

Revelation 22:17

Without that union, intimacy or marriage, we have nothing but religion; an empty form that does not produce life or eternal fruit.

That is why Jesus prayed to the Father that we would be one, in the Father and in Him, so the world would believe in Him.

that they all may be one, as You, Father, are in Me, and I in You; that they also may be one in Us, that the world may believe that You sent Me.

John 17:21

The understanding and the life that flows from this golden bowl, from this marriage bed, connects us in true unity with other Sons of God whose golden bowls are also full of God. We fellowship with them in a genuine way and our unity is not based on theologies, organizations or common projects, but on the Spirit of God that flows from one to another.

God is not divided, and those who are Sons of God are true brothers. Our union was established even before the foundation of the world, and here, we simply recognize each other. We do not know them according to the flesh, but according to the Spirit, in the same way we know the Lord Jesus.

Therefore, from now on, we regard no one according to the flesh. Even though we have known Christ according to the flesh, yet now we know Him thus no longer.

2 Corinthians 5:16

Our spirit bubbles within us when we meet on the earth, as if we knew each other from eternity. This is God, which recognizes Himself in one another.

In this the children of God and the children of the devil are manifest: Whoever does not practice righteousness is not of God, nor is he who does not love his brother.

1 John 3:10

We know that we have passed from death to life, because we love the brethren. He who does not love his brother abides in death.

Whoever hates his brother is a murderer, and you know that no murderer has eternal life abiding in him.

By this we know love, because He laid down His life for us. And we also ought to lay down our lives for the brethren.

1 John 3:14-16

We have grown so used to seeing ourselves according to what divides us. The reality is, everything that divides us is flesh, because we do not know how to operate by the Spirit, through understanding our own spirit as well as God's.

The Golden Bowl is the fountain of love that unites and connects everyone who is His.

Sometimes I allow the life and the love that flows from my golden bowl to touch the souls of those who do not know God. In those places where it is not easy to open my mouth and preach, I simply sit and allow the water to flow from my spirit and begin to embrace and love the dormant spirits of those around me.

They do not even know what is happening to them, but divine light is illuminating them, filling them with peace or faith. It could be that the person who had never prayed before, not knowing why, suddenly prays to God, or cries out to him or thanks Him. Maybe they begin to feel a desire to repent of their sins and change their lives. Without uttering a single word, our spirit, united with God, makes His glorious presence palpable, filling the atmosphere.

Figure 7 - The River of God flowing from The Golden Bowl

Chapter 6

THE PITCHER, THE FOUNTAIN AND THE WELL

... before the silver cord is loosed, or the golden bowl is broken, or the pitcher shattered at the fountain, or the wheel at the well.

Ecclesiastes 12:6

1. The Pitcher and The Fountain

The pitcher is the container, or the vessel that shapes the soul of man. The fountain is God Himself, and the well is the heart. Just like the life of God is deposited into the golden bowl, the soul is contained in a spiritual vessel. This pitcher is joined together with the spirit through ligaments that interconnect, and they both share an intermediate organ, which is the heart. The pitcher of the soul encompasses the entire form of our body, as it will also impart vital energy to the entire organism.

Later on in this study, we will analyze these interconnections as well as the heart. What I want you to see in this moment is how our internal being is linked in all its parts.

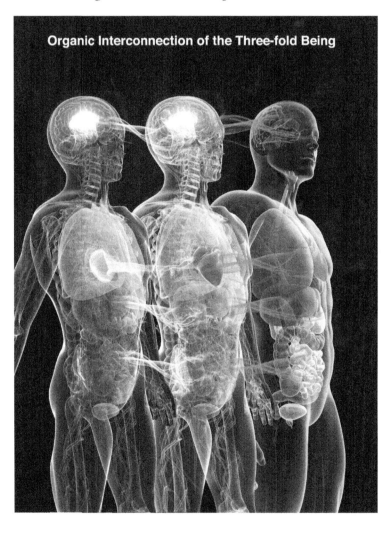

Figure 8 - Interconnections between the Spirit, Soul and Body

Let us continue analyzing the different parts mentioned in the Book of Ecclesiastes.

When the Lord began to reveal the anatomy of our being to me, He led me in a vision to understand a singular perspective in the dialogue between Jesus and the Samaritan woman at Jacob's well.

In the vision, Jesus represented the fountain of life within the golden bowl and He was offering the living waters of the Spirit to the pitcher or soul, represented in the woman.

This dialogue had always seemed very strange to me, because if it is looked at in the natural, one cannot make heads or tails of it. They jump from one topic to another without coherence.

It was extraordinary to hear this conversation from a different point of view; the spirit and the soul talking to one another.

We will now see how the story develops taking that point of view. Let us go to the Gospel of John Chapter 4:6-26 and I will paraphrase the dialogue of the Spirit and how the soul responds.

The Spirit - The Fountain - must break the pitcher to cause the birth of a new creature.

> *Now Jacob's well was there. Jesus therefore, being wearied from His journey, sat thus by the well. It was about the sixth hour.*
>
> *A woman of Samaria came to draw water. Jesus said to her, "Give Me a drink."*   *John 4:6-7*

The Spirit of God (Jesus) comes to the heart of man (well) and the thirsty soul (Samaritan woman) also comes to this place, from where she always extracts what encourages her, and where she seeks to be satisfied.

The Spirit, intending for the soul to recognize her lack, and inability to quench the thirst within her heart, challenged her to give Him a drink.

> *Then the woman of Samaria said to Him, "How is it that You, being a Jew, ask a drink from me, a Samaritan woman?" For Jews have no dealings with Samaritans.*
>
> *John 4:9*

The carnal soul and mind, being enemies of the Spirit, and being used to reject what could come out of it, respond with logical reasoning.

> *Jesus answered and said to her, "If you knew the gift of God, and who it is who says to you, 'Give Me a drink,' you would have asked Him, and He would have given you living water."*
>
> *John 4:10*

The Spirit, patient as always, illuminates the understanding of the soul by letting her know there are things that have been granted from God that she is unaware of. The soul is awakened in her curiosity, and in her desire to know the mysteries she has been unable to figure out. Now she has a new thirst, something she has never heard of and this has intrigued her: living water?

"What is that like?" she asks herself. The Spirit does not have all these formulas, programs and scriptures that have satisfied me throughout my life, she thinks. What does He plan to use to contain the water if he does not have a container to retain it, so it will not scatter? I have only been able to quench my thirst with water that I am able to store and control, and He proposes living water that is better than the one in my bucket?

The woman said to Him, "Sir, You have nothing to draw with, and the well is deep. Where then do You get that living water?

Are You greater than our father Jacob, who gave us the well, and drank from it himself, as well as his sons and his livestock?"   *John 4:11-12*

The soul, religious by nature, always hangs on to what she is familiar with, what her parents taught her, as well as traditions. That is where she feels secure. This is her first line of defense in resisting the life of the Spirit, which is impalpable and uncontainable, unprecedented and unfathomable. She is terrified of what she cannot control or manage.

But the Spirit is alive and is touching the most sensitive fibers of the soul. It is bringing her out of balance in order for her to see her true and eternal need.

Finally, the soul begins to give in, and a new line of questioning emerges from within. My heart is deep and full of needs, she concludes. It is a deep well, unfathomable, full of caves and hidden corners I only have access to. How can someone go into these remote places in my inner being and extract something that quenches my thirst? But … in all honesty, I am getting tired of coming to this well and still being thirsty all the time, she concludes.

Jesus answered and said to her, "Whoever drinks of this water will thirst again,

but whoever drinks of the water that I shall give him will never thirst. But the water that I shall give him will become in him a fountain of water springing up into everlasting life."

The woman said to Him, "Sir, give me this water, that I may not thirst, nor come here to draw." John 4:13-15

The Spirit skillfully interrupts that cycle of internal questioning and reveals Himself to the soul. What comes out of His mouth is alive and reconnects the soul to eternity. This one word causes her whole anemic being to shake at the very second it touches her origin and destiny. This is the bait that traps her and causes the light of hope to shine upon her most terrible fear: death. This is the tormentor that has directed her all of her life and has had her under his serfdom. Suddenly she realizes that this tormentor is not in control of her life as she had always thought he was. She realizes that she needs something that genuinely leads her to the eternal truths so she will never thirst again. Humbling herself before her inability, she finally asks the Spirit, "Give me this water."

> *Jesus said to her, "Go, call your husband, and come here."*
>
> *The woman answered and said, "I have no husband." Jesus said to her, "You have well said, 'I have no husband,'*
>
> *for you have had five husbands, and the one whom you now have is not your husband; in that you spoke truly."*
>
> *John 4:16-18*

Everything seemed to indicate that she had gone to the right place to receive living water, but the willingness of the soul to long for something from the Spirit, was not enough for Him to just give it to her.

The soul, in her longing to satisfy her primary needs of existence, marries to different ideals. She thinks to herself, what truly satisfies me? She then decides that if she finds true love and has a family that it will bring happiness. However, as time passes, she realizes that even though it is a great blessing, there is still an emptiness that leaves her unsatisfied.

She then chases another ideal and marries it. I will have lots of money! She obtains it with great effort, but comes to the conclusion that the more she accumulates and spends; she grows more and more bored.

She then decides to marry a third ideal, something much more important than money; fame, recognition and success. She obtains it with great effort and the world applauds her big name. Her name and her titles are on the doors of buildings and streets but she still comes to the same conclusion. True satisfaction of the soul is not there either.

She then thinks about doing something humanitarian. She longs to feel like a hero, a true altruist that loves the poor and the needy. But she does not quench her thirst with this either. All of this has done nothing but inflate her "ego" and which she has fed with all these things.

The last attempt of the soul is the one she considers the most sublime, and decides to become a servant of God.

She learns all the religious concepts and graduates from the top theological university. She learns to pray with understanding, to worship with established songs and to write the best sermons. She has all the answers according to the counseling manual to help her followers.

In the end all she has is an empty form, but not the essence. She calls God, "her husband," and even though in the bottom of her soul she knows there is something more she has not yet reached, she does not have the strength or the motivation to change. She has filled herself with so many formulas and religious vocabulary that she knows differs from the reality of her life. The problem is that it is too painful for the soul to admit that everything that derives from her is dead works. It is heartbreaking for her to think that her own acts of righteousness look as filthy rags before God.

But we are all like an unclean thing, and all our righteousnesses are like filthy rags; we all fade as a leaf, and our iniquities, like the wind, have taken us away.

Isaiah 64:6

The soul that has filled herself with religiosity is the most difficult to be touched and transformed by the Spirit of Life, but nothing impossible for God.

It is precisely there when the Spirit bursts in and knocks on the door of the heart. "For you have had five husbands, and the one whom you now have is not your husband."

But…"Jesus is my husband!" exclaims the religious soul. I sing you love songs and serve in church every day. Isn't that what you request from me?

The Spirit then responds: You are married to many things, many man made theologies, and traditions I never established. My Spirit cannot be fused with yours until you leave all those husbands and consecrate yourself to me so you can know me as I am, and how I have conceived you. Only then can I give you the Water of Life.

The soul then humbles herself and says, "The one whom I now have is not my husband."

The soul has now recognized its thirst, its spiritual state, but even then, her religious structures continue to argue with the Spirit. The soul is focused on the earth: Where is the actual physical place I should worship? She wanders.

> *The woman said to Him, "Sir, I perceive that You are a prophet.*
>
> *Our fathers worshiped on this mountain, and you Jews say that in Jerusalem is the place where one ought to worship."* John 4:19-20

Jesus had come to establish a Kingdom in the Spirit. The dispensation of the soul subject to the law, fulfilling forms and physical ordinances had come to an end. Now, the union between God and man would be established and God would make Himself known through the Spirit, not through works, but through grace and through faith.

The soul always looks to the things of the earth and the earthly Jerusalem. But, the Spirit opens her understanding and tells her, that times have changed and what was important in other generations will now be exchanged. The important thing will no longer be the natural realm but the Spirit, which is the essence of God.

The soul has a difficult time understanding what Jesus said about worship will no longer be in Jerusalem; because the soul is religious and earthly by nature. This does not mean there aren't godly people worshipping in the Holy Land. What He meant was that the center of worship was no longer going to be in the earthly realm, but in the spiritual.

77

Jesus said to her, "Woman, believe Me, the hour is coming when you will neither on this mountain, nor in Jerusalem, worship the Father.

You worship what you do not know; we know what we worship, for salvation is of the Jews.

But the hour is coming, and now is, when the true worshipers will worship the Father in spirit and truth; for the Father is seeking such to worship Him.

God is Spirit, and those who worship Him must worship in spirit and truth."   *John 4:21-24*

The Spirit speaks to the soul about how this Water of Life manifests. First, it comes from our interior and then it exteriorizes in the form of spontaneous and prophetic worship. The Spirit says: It is necessary that you worship this way, in spirit, and through a soul that is aligned with the truth. He does not give an option for other types of worship.

The Spirit takes us into the introspection in which He took the Samaritan woman in order to convert us into true worshippers. Then this worship will flow out from the golden bowl.

Every one of us must be converted into those trees planted by the Lord, by His river, producing the sound of waters that springs forth in true worship. We are the planting of God, but we are also the river. When we gather to worship in this way, united by the Spirit, we become dozens and hundreds and thousands of streams of life that produce the sound of many waters where Jesus, the King of Kings manifests in His Glory.

*And I heard, as it were, the voice of a **great multitude, as the sound of many waters** and as the sound of mighty thunderings, saying, "Alleluia! For the Lord God Omnipotent reigns!*

Revelation 19:6

and in the midst of the seven lampstands One like the Son of Man, clothed with a garment down to the feet and girded about the chest with a golden band.

His head and hair were white like wool, as white as snow, and His eyes like a flame of fire;

His feet were like fine brass, as if refined in a furnace, and His voice as the sound of many waters;

Revelation 1:13-15

When the rivers are flowing from our interior, it is the Living water of the Voice of Jesus in His Glory that is heard. The soul is arrested and enveloped in this presence. The Body of Christ unites and the waters flow out of the auditoriums and homes to touch the cities and cause everything to be vivified through the waters.

The Sons of God become lush trees, full of the fruit of the Spirit. The spiritual brightness and splendor emanating from them are their leaves which heal the bodies and the city. No written song, no matter how beautiful or inspirational it may be, can produce the life and the impact of the worship that comes down from Heaven and ascends to Him once again. The angels join in, as well as all the choirs in Heaven.

The woman said to Him, "I know that Messiah is coming" (who is called Christ). "When He comes, He will tell us all things." John 4:25

The soul cannot recognize the Messiah on its own. He is right in front of her and she is not able to discern it. Only the spirit is able to recognize The Son of God and understand His Presence in her inner being and in her worship. Only the spirit who has been born of God can recognize His Kingdom and Majesty. They are in the midst of us, here and now.

The soul cannot receive the Spirit of the Messiah in herself; it is the spirit which receives it. She can only surrender to His Lordship.

This is why religion, which is formed as a structure within her soul, causes her to feel like she cannot reach God. Even with Christ manifesting right in front of her, because of her inability to perceive Him, she will always seek something different; something external that makes her feel that He is the Messiah she was waiting for.

The spirit seeks the internal where God abides with man and where Heaven and Earth are united. The soul, either surrenders to the ruling of the spirit, or will remain waiting without ever experiencing the Glory of God, which is Jesus Christ.

The dialogue between the Spirit and the soul culminates when Jesus says:

Jesus said to her, "I who speak to you am He."

John 4:26

And Jesus is speaking to your soul right now. I am the one speaking to you. Listen to what I want to do in your spirit, and he who has ears to hear, hear.

> *teaching them to observe all, whatever I did command you,) and lo, I am with you all the days -- till the full end of the age.'*
>
> *Matthew 28:20 YLT[5]*

2. The Well, the Heart of Man

The heart is one of the most important parts of our inner being and is the door that connects the spirit and soul. The comprehension of this spiritual organ opens up an extensive gamut of concepts and ramifications. For this reason, I will not deviate from the analysis of the spirit right now, but will leave the study of the heart for later on in the book (Chapter 9).

[5] Young's Literal Translation, Public Domain

Chapter 7

THE WHEELS OF THE SPIRIT

... before the silver cord is loosed, or the golden bowl is broken, or the pitcher shattered at the fountain, or the wheel at the well.

Ecclesiastes 12:6

1. The Design of the Universe

The entire universe is held together by circles of energy. These exert a centripetal pressure or a gravitational force that maintains everything in place and in the form God intended. From the elemental structure of the atom, to all solar systems and galaxies in space everything is contained by these gravitational rings.

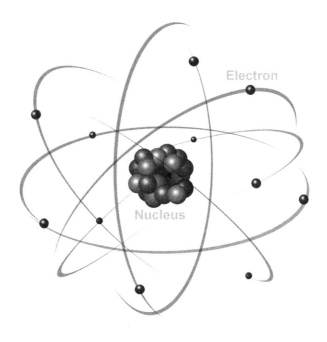

Figure 9 - Basic Structure of the Atom

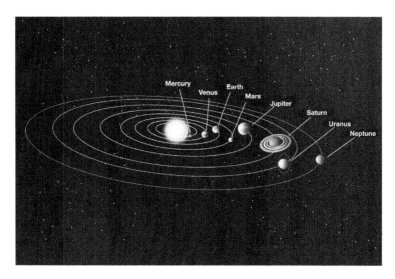

Figure 10 - Planetary System

The same is true in the invisible realm. The substance every spirit is composed of is volatile and ethereal. Therefore, it needs something to surround it and allow it to preserve its form and physiognomy. This is why it needs these wheels. If our spirits or that of angels and other heavenly or demonic creatures would not have these wheels of energy around them, they would vaporize.

2. The Throne of God, the Basic Unity of Creation

The Throne of God is the unit from where the entire universe is sustained and governed. Everything takes His form, whether visible or invisible. This is the primary unit, which is "All in All," from where all laws that maintain creation in order, emerge.

While scientists have identified these forces and measured them as energy, velocity, gravity, et cetera, they have never been able to figure out what they are, or where they come from. This is logical, because they do not dare to state that it is the power of the God of the universe.

However, the Sons of God have been given the understanding of the Mysteries of the Almighty.

There is something very interesting in the book of Daniel, which states that the Throne of God is surrounded by wheels of fire. God, in His omnipresent nature is in every place, and goes on even further than all galaxies, universes and dimensions of the Spirit. But, when He chooses to make Himself visible to the eyes of our spirit and to the myriads of angels, living creatures and the perfected spirits of the saints, He then appears surrounded by wheels of fire.

*"I watched till thrones were put in place, and the
Ancient of Days was seated; His garment was white as
snow, and the hair of His head was like pure wool. His
throne was a fiery flame, its wheels a burning fire;*

*A fiery stream issued and came forth from before Him.
A thousand thousands ministered to Him; Ten thousand
times ten thousand stood before Him. The court was
seated, and the books were opened.*

Daniel 7:9-10

If God is the unit everything precedes from, then that will be
reflected in creation, whether physical or spiritual.

If I translate this into scientific language, it is described as follows:
Every atom has an energy nucleus that is contained by circles or
wheels of electrons. Through the force of gravity they keep the
atom united, and produce an electromagnetic field which
emanates from the inside out. This is true inside an atom, in a
solar system and in all beings, living and spiritual.

Our spirit is God's life, His very breath inside of us, to make us
in His image and likeness. In this manner, His throne is among
us in the "Golden Bowl," also surrounded by wheels, and with His
river flowing out of us.

Figure 11 - The Throne of God surrounded by Wheels of Fire

The word of God also shows how creation is contained within a wheel, and within it, there are millions upon millions of wheels within wheels.

The main wheels surround the throne of God, and everything is created from there and is interconnected. If we could see the united body of Christ linked by its joints, from an energy point of view, it would be millions of intertwined wheels.

> *And the tongue is a fire: the world of iniquity among our members is the tongue, which defileth the whole body, and setteth on fire the **wheel of nature**, and is set on fire by hell.*
>
> *James 3:6 ASV*

3. The Spirit is inside the Wheels

When Prophet Ezekiel had the vision of the living creatures, he clearly saw these wheels which contained them and moved with them.

The appearance of the wheels and their workings was like the color of beryl, and all four had the same likeness. The appearance of their workings was, as it were, a wheel in the middle of a wheel.

When they moved, they went toward any one of four directions; they did not turn aside when they went.

As for their rims, they were so high they were awesome; and their rims were full of eyes, all around the four of them.

When the living creatures went, the wheels went beside them; and when the living creatures were lifted up from the earth, the wheels were lifted up. Wherever the spirit wanted to go, they went, because there the spirit went; and the wheels were lifted together with them, for the spirit of the living creatures was in the wheels.

Ezekiel 1:16-20

Figure 12 - Living Creature in Ezekiel's Vision

4. The Wheels' Functions

a. Translation by the Spirit

These wheels not only contained the spirit of the living creatures, but they also transported them from one place to another.

Jesus told Nicodemus, those born of God were like the wind. The wind represents the spirit, and as mentioned before, is the only element out of the four others, that is not connected to the earth. That is why those born of the spirit have entered a "glorious freedom." Their spirits are free and can enter into all the dimensions God has granted them, as their inheritance. They are guided by the Spirit of God like a leaf blown by the wind.

While the spirit of man is in a state of death or dormant, the wheels are inactive in their functions and only serve to keep the spirit from losing its form. Once the golden bowl has been filled by Jesus Christ, and our spirit has been born again, it becomes the seat and temple of The Most High. Its wheels are activated by the wheels of the Throne in order to move and operate in the Kingdom of God.

Jesus answered, "Most assuredly, I say to you, unless one is born of water and the Spirit, he cannot enter the kingdom of God.

John 3:5

The wheels allow us to change dimensions. I believe these were the wheels of fire that descended from the Throne of God that caught up Enoch and Elijah. Enoch simply entered the heavenly realm and disappeared from the earth. Elisha saw the chariots of fire, the horses and the whirlwind that took Elijah his teacher. These three are spiritual forms that have to do with movement and interdimensional translation.

Elijah was taken from one place to another during his ministry. He had the same ability as the living creatures Ezekiel described. They were able to fly from one place to another and the wheels with them, this same thing happened to Elijah.

I want you to notice this in the way the next scripture is written. This is the moment Elijah supernaturally appeared to Obadiah, head servant of King Ahab, as he was looking for him.

And it came to pass after many days that the word of the Lord came to Elijah, in the third year, saying, "Go, present yourself to Ahab, and I will send rain on the earth." ...

And Ahab had called Obadiah, who was in charge of his house. (Now Obadiah feared the Lord greatly. ...)

Now as Obadiah was on his way, suddenly Elijah met him; and he recognized him, and fell on his face, and said, "Is that you, my lord Elijah?"

And he answered him, "It is I. Go, tell your master, 'Elijah is here.'"

1 Kings 18:1; 3; 7-8

The servant, knowing Elijah's reputation of appearing and disappearing answers:

*And it shall come to pass, as soon as I am gone from you, that **the Spirit of the Lord will carry you to a place I do not know**; so when I go and tell Ahab, and he cannot find you, he will kill me. But I your servant have feared the Lord from my youth.*

1 Kings 18:12

These words make it clear that Elijah was known for being taken by God and translated to other places. Now, it is impossible for Elijah in the natural, to know where to find Obadiah in the exact moment that King Ahab was looking for him.

But the Spirit of Jehovah, who had ordered the Prophet to present himself before the King was the one who translated him to the place where the servant could be found.

Jesus said that the least in the Kingdom of Heaven was greater than all the prophets and He also said that the violent take the truth of the Kingdom of God by force[6].

We can see there were disciples that took ownership of this faculty of the spirit. Among them was Phillip, who was transported from one place to another[7] and Paul the Apostle was transported through the jail doors[8]. Also, both Apostles Paul and John were taken to Paradise and to the third heaven and to diverse heavenly places[9].

This tells me that we can long for the greatest gifts, and this is one we can receive. This power is within the wheels of the spirit.

---

[6] Assuredly, I say to you, among those born of women there has not risen one greater than John the Baptist; but he who is least in the kingdom of heaven is greater than he. And from the days of John the Baptist until now the kingdom of heaven suffers violence, and the violent take it by force. (Matthew 11:11-12)

[7] Now when they came up out of the water, the Spirit of the Lord caught Philip away, so that the eunuch saw him no more; and he went on his way rejoicing. (Acts 8:39)

[8] When they were past the first and the second guard posts, they came to the iron gate that leads to the city, which opened to them of its own accord; and they went out and went down one street, and immediately the angel departed from him. (Acts 12:10)

[9] I know a man in Christ who fourteen years ago—whether in the body I do not know, or whether out of the body I do not know, God knows—such a one was caught up to the third heaven. (2 Corinthians 12:2)

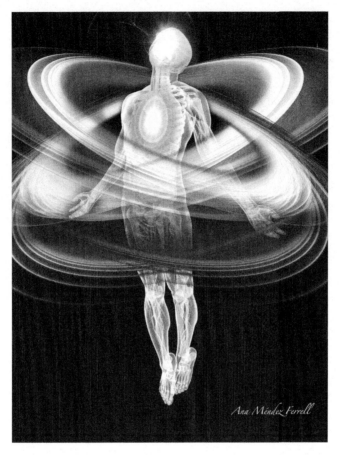

Figure 13 - The Wheels of the Spirit

When God showed me the vision of our spirit, I marveled at the sight of these wheels. Little by little, the Holy Spirit began to teach me their functions.

The first function I learned was the one I just mentioned, the ability to be transported or translated from one place to another. God has allowed us to experience this several times when we have been taken to certain places that are two to four hours away, in a matter of seconds.

There have been times when we have climbed very high mountains to consecrate them to God, and we have asked God to translate us to help us in the more dangerous areas and have seen this miracle several times.

It is written in the book of Isaiah:

> *Arise, shine; for your light has come! And the glory of the Lord is risen upon you.*
>
> *For behold, the darkness shall cover the earth, and deep darkness the people; But the Lord will arise over you, and His glory will be seen upon you,*
>
> *. . .*
>
> *"Who are these who **fly like a cloud**, And like doves to their roosts?*
>
> Isaiah 60:1-2; 8

> *With a noise like chariots over mountaintops **they leap, like the noise of a flaming fire** that devours the stubble, like a strong people set in battle array.*
>
> Joel 2:5

To be taken by the Spirit and do things that eyes have not seen, nor ears have not heard, is part of our inheritance when we enter the Glory of His Kingdom.

An Experience that changed my Life

When God allowed us to climb Mount Everest to liberate the "*10-40 Window*"[10], we underwent an eight-month express mountain climbing training, since no one in our team was a mountain climber.

During this time we all dreamed of the moment when we would reach the summit in order to consecrate the altitudes of the earth to our God. Although the goal was a leading from the Holy Spirit, my human and carnal heart longed for my name to go down in history as the first latin woman to reach the summit of the earth. God not only had us lay our life down onto death, since this was a killer mountain, but I also had to lay down this desire to reach the summit unto the altar of God. The human glory of having done something incredible was carnal arrogance deep inside.

Mountains, among other things are a symbol of the traits of human pride, as well as what we can get in our own strength. We could not defeat the spiritual stronghold that was there, if we did not deal with that part of our heart.

When we began the expedition, God confirmed that we would not reach the summit[11] since the center of power was not there, but rather in an area that was around 21,000 feet[11] high.

We were approaching base camp and our last stop before arriving was close to a mountain named Kala Patthar (approximately 18,000 feet high). We had walked about twelve hours and almost everyone was exhausted. However, Veronica[12], one of our intercessors and I were supernaturally filled with energy.

---

[10] Zone between the line of Latitude 10 and 40, which was the least evangelized zone in the world in the 1990s.

[11] Mount Everest's Summit is at 8,848 meters /29,029 ft above sea level.

[12] Verónica Cabrera from México D.F. (Mexico City)

In that moment God placed in our hearts the imperative desire to climb Kala Patthar. The command seemed strange to us, but we felt a fire that drove us, so having consulted with our authority, we began the ascent.

During the eight days journey towards Everest base camp, the skies had been cloudy so we had not been able to see Everest, not even in close proximity. That afternoon was the exception. When we arrived at the summit of this other mountain, we came across what seemed to be a bed of stone as if it was an ancient place where sacrifices took place yet this one had not been carved by man.

We felt the Lord was telling us to lie down and lay down in that altar-like place all desire for glory resulting from human effort. We did just that. In that moment the clouds opened and the peak of Everest appeared before us for the first time, golden like a diamond of fire, illuminated by the warm tint of the setting sun.

When we saw it for the first time we could not help but weep out of excitement and pain at the same time, because we knew we would not get to step on the summit.

We closed our eyes and placed our crown and our mission at the feet of the Lord.

Our greatest satisfaction was for Him to receive all the Glory in all things. Thinking of this made us feel very happy, even more so, than if we had reached the goal every mountain climber has.

The Holy Spirit then came upon us with great power and His Glory enveloped us. We stopped feeling the weight of our bodies; we were weightless and captivated in a radiant light. I knew on the inside that God was taking the expedition for Himself and orchestrating everything so that it would be Him and only Him that would be seated in the heights of the earth. Suddenly, we were no longer on the bed of stone. We do not know how much time went by, but when we opened our eyes we saw something that left us speechless.

We were standing on the summit of Everest. We looked at each other, unable to understand this wonder. We then gave God the glory. Our names were never registered in human records and we would never be tempted to glorify ourselves, as if we had accomplished something through our own effort. Days later the Lord in all His Glory sat on the heights of the earth, and this is what will always be remembered.

As for us, we will always be grateful for this experience that changed our lives. As the Apostle Paul would say:

> *I know a man in Christ who fourteen years ago—whether in the body I do not know, or whether out of the body I do not know, God knows—such a one was caught up to the third heaven.*
>
> *And I know such a man—whether in the body or out of the body I do not know, God knows—*
>
> *how he was caught up into Paradise and heard inexpressible words, which it is not lawful for a man to utter.*
>
> *Of such a one I will boast;* **yet of myself I will not boast, except in my infirmities***.*
>
> *2 Corinthians 12:2-5*

Experiences such as these should always lead us to the feet of Jesus and not to our own exaltation. If I dared to share this, it is because I feel the freedom of the Spirit to do so, and my intention is to help you understand and believe the things God can do with you. As for me, I have kept this to myself for 18 years and I choose, like Paul the Apostle, to glory in my weaknesses.

b. The Ability of the Wheels to elevate our Spirit

When the Lord began to show me the functions of the wheels, I realized that not only could we be transported physically or spiritually, but we could be elevated in the dimensions of the Spirit.

> *Who are these who **fly like a cloud,** and like doves to their roosts?*
>
> *Isaiah 60:8*

Clouds are formed when vapor that rises from the ocean or other bodies of water, condensates.

This transformation water goes through when it converts into a weightless element. It is similar to what happens to our spirit when it is elevated into the heavenly dimensions of the Kingdom of God.

The wheels of our spirit are in continuous movement, and this produces a certain frequency. This is the scientific term used to measure light, sound, and electromagnetic fields, and it determines how compact or elongated the waves are produced by these forces.

The frequencies of these wheels increase as the wheels spin faster. As this frequency keeps on increasing, it causes our spirit to be elevated into higher dimensions than those of the earth. I use the term elevate because it is the sensation we experience when we are tuning ourselves into the spiritual world. That is why it is written:

> *Arise, shine; for your light has come!*
>
> *Isaiah 60:1*

When the light and the Glory of Christ envelopes our spirit and fills it with Him, the wheels begin to spin at an extraordinary speed and we are elevated like vapor that rises to the sky.

In the presence of God, which produces this acceleration of the wheels, and in a more intense immersing in His Spirit, we will reach a higher dimension each time.

When John the Apostle was on the Island of Patmos, he said, "I was in the Spirit"[13]. He was in that place of stillness, where our spirit begins to tune itself and enter into communion with the Spirit of God. It is in that place, when we quiet our mind, our worries and open the door of our spirit, so the presence of God can flow from our golden bowl.

Since John entered into that state, his wheels began to spin at a great speed. His spirit was at the same frequency as heaven, and could now see Jesus Christ in His glorified body.

It is the same as the propeller of an airplane. When it spins at a great speed, it becomes invisible to our eyes, but if we take a picture with a digital camera we will see the blades. That is because digital cameras can capture objects that spin at extraordinary frequencies.

The same takes place in the spirit realm. The Kingdom of God has a very high frequency, it speeds extremely rapidly and when our wheels are spinning at low levels or earthly levels, we cannot see it. When we worship in Spirit and in Truth or we enter the stillness of the Spirit, the wheels change our frequency and the invisible world becomes visible.

John, having seen the glorious revelation of Jesus Christ and having received the message of the seven letters of the book of

---

[13] I was in the Spirit on the Lord's Day, and I heard behind me a loud voice, as of a trumpet. (Revelation 1:10)

Revelation, said something very interesting. Notice that he was still "in the Spirit" when he looked up and saw a heavenly door.

> *After these things I looked, and behold, a door standing open in heaven. And the first voice which I heard was like a trumpet speaking with me, saying, "Come up here, and I will show you things which must take place after this."*
>
> *Immediately I was in the Spirit; and behold, a throne set in heaven, and One sat on the throne.*
>
> *Revelation 4:1-2*

Then, being already "in the Spirit", he is taken to another spiritual dimension, a higher level on the other side of the door. At that moment, the wheels increased his frequency and took him to where God was calling him.

The different dimensions of heaven have doors or thresholds, where we can see and experience deeper and multiple things of God.

c. The Elasticity of the Wheels

The spiritual world is not subject to time, space or the three dimensions of the physical world. Understanding this is vital, since attempting to understand the Kingdom of God with its different planes and depths from the limits of our universe, is a big error.

We measure with the metric decimal system or in pounds or feet, or many other measurements that have to do with something physical. Heaven and its dimensions have very different measurements.

We can measure two dimensions by the calculating of height and width. We can measure a third, by adding the concept of depth. But, how can we measure the fourth, fifth or tenth dimension with the measurements of a physical and material world?

When we speak of heavenly things we will run into phrases such as these:

> *Then he measured its wall: one hundred and forty-four cubits, according to the measure of a man, that is, of an angel.*
>
> *Revelation 21:17*

> *Then I was given a reed like a measuring rod. And the angel stood, saying, "Rise and measure the temple of God, the altar, and those who worship there.*
>
> *Revelation 11:1*

Why does God ask him to measure the Temple and the Altar, if God gave the measurements to King David? How can you measure worshippers? They can be counted, but can they be measured?

The truth is the mechanics to measure spiritual dimensions have nothing to do with our earthly concept of measuring something.

What I am alluding to is that we must understand that the spiritual world has an elasticity that allows heavenly things to expand or be restrained as needed.

God, for example, who is omnipresent and occupies all space, can reduce Himself to make His dwelling within man. All of Heaven, the New Jerusalem, and the Throne of God can all dwell in one individual.

We sometimes read that God is so large that the Earth, in all its immensity, is only His footstool.

'Heaven is My throne, and earth is My footstool. What house will you build for Me? says the Lord, or what is the place of My rest?

Acts 7:49

That would, however make Him smaller than our solar system. He says He rides upon a cherub on the wings of the wind, but it is obvious that He is not as small as a cherub. While on the subject, I'll take this opportunity to clarify that cherubs are high ranking angels placed in charge of watching over the Glory of God. They are not the small headed creatures with wings men have placed on religious paintings.

He bowed the heavens also, and came down with darkness under His feet. And He rode upon a cherub, and flew; He flew upon the wings of the wind.

Psalms 18:9-10

What I want you to notice is in the spiritual world, measurements are not restricted like they are in the physical world. I had an experience that opened my understanding regarding the elasticity of our spirit.

I was in prayer preparing myself for spiritual warfare against the terrible spirits of witchcraft that governed Mexico. At the time, I lived on the twelfth floor of a modern building. It had large windows that went down to the floor and when standing close to them, one could experience vertigo.

While praying, I stood so close that I could see the pavement as if I was practically in the air. In that moment, the Lord asked me a question. *"How many ants do you see on the pavement in front of the building?"* The question seemed very strange since it was impossible to see something like that from the twelfth floor, so I answered with all honesty: "None, Lord. If there are ants there, they are too small for me to see them."

As I was saying this, I saw my spirit grow, and I literally saw myself like a giant standing on the pavement. Then the Lord said to me: *"The size of those ants is the size of your enemies. Your spirit is as large as you want it to be, or as small as you need it to be."*

In that instant, my spirit grew and became as large as the city of Mexico, and the Lord said: *"Cover the city with your spirit and release the Spirit of Resurrection upon it, like Elisha did with the child that had died."* It is awesome to understand the power we have, united with the Spirit of God.

The wheels are the ones that give us the ability to grow and shrink. Sometimes we need to be very small or invisible to pass by undetected in the enemy's camp or to speak in a person's ear.

Chapter 8

ORGANS, SYSTEMS AND FUNCTIONS OF THE SPIRIT

We have now seen the external part of our spirit, and how it is seen at first sight, with the golden bowl, the silver cord and its wheels. We will now go to the innermost part, where we find the different organs within our spirit.

1. The Seven Spirits of God

When John the Apostle saw Jesus in all His Glory, he saw Him among seven golden lampstands. These lampstands are very important in order to understand life, light and how our innermost being works, because everything the second Adam's image is, is what needs to be quickened in our spirit.

Jesus is the life of everything created and the substance our spirit. Every spirit comes from God and returns to God who gave it[14].

---

[14] Ecclesiastes 12:7

By Him all things consist, and in Him we live and move and have our being. That life, as described in the Gospel of John is the light of man[15]. The life of Jesus Christ is what illuminates us to have understanding in our spirit.

When the Tabernacle of Moses was erected, the only piece of furniture that had light was the lampstand with seven arms located in the Holy Place. This symbolized the Holy Spirit, which would be inside every believer after Pentecost.

That is why Jesus moves among the seven lampstands. It means that the Holy Spirit is the one who makes His church live.

Jesus is where the church of His design is.

> *Then I turned to see the voice that spoke with me. And having turned I saw seven golden lampstands, and in the midst of the seven lampstands*
>
> *One like the Son of Man, clothed with a garment down to the feet and girded about the chest with a golden band.*
>
> *...*
>
> *The mystery of the seven stars which you saw in My right hand, and the seven golden lampstands: The seven stars are the angels of the seven churches, and the seven lampstands which you saw are the seven churches.*
>
> *Revelation 1:12-13; 20*

Now, what is true for the body is true for each one of its members. If the life of the Church is in its lampstand, then our spirit also has its own.

---

[15] In Him was life; and the life was the light of men. (John 1:4)

The Spirit of God diffracts or manifests itself in The seven Spirits of God and they are a part of Jesus in His Glory.

They are described in the vision John has of the Throne, in the book of Revelation, as eyes in the midst of The Lamb. The horns represent His absolute Lordship, while the eyes represent the impact of His Spirit upon all the earth.

> *And I looked, and behold, in the midst of the throne and of the four living creatures, and in the midst of the elders, stood a Lamb as though it had been slain, having seven horns and seven eyes, which are the seven Spirits of God sent out into all the earth.*
>
> *Revelation 5:6*

The Power of His Spirit and the broad gamut of what He Is, are our inheritance, and the internal configuration of who we are.

What the second Adam has is what we children of God have, being born from His genetics and His Spirit.

> *The Spirit of the Lord shall rest upon Him, **the Spirit of wisdom and understanding, the Spirit of counsel and might, the Spirit of knowledge and of the fear of the Lord.***
>
> *Isaiah 11:2*

> *And from the Throne proceeded lightnings, thunderings, and voices. Seven lamps of fire were burning before the throne, which are the seven Spirits of God.*
>
> *Revelation 4:5*

These seven spirits come to us when Jesus comes to dwell in our lives. However, they are not activated immediately. They begin to ignite as we develop our spirit, allowing Christ to be formed in us.

My little children, for whom I labor in birth again until Christ is formed in you,

Galatians 4:19

If we could see our spirit from the top of our head, we could see the seven lamps located around the golden bowl.

As it is shown in the diagram, the Spirit of the Lord is found at the center of the area of communion. Around it is the conscience (circular area which encloses the flames), wrapped by the wheels of the Spirit (exterior circle). The lamp of the Fear of The Lord rests next to the conscience and is intertwined with wisdom. On the other side, knowledge, intelligence and counsel are interconnected, while the Power of God emanates from the inside out.

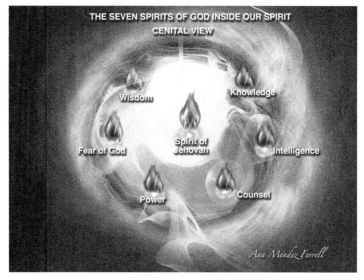

Figure 14 - Ignited Lamps within a completely vivified Spirit

Every one of the seven spirits governs and illuminates one or several parts of the spirit, which we will refer to as "organs of the spirit."

2. The Anatomy of The Spirit of Man

We will now enter into a marvelous part of our study, where we will be analyzing the whole internal configuration of our spirit.

The following illustration is a drawing where I intended to project the vision of the spirit of man God gave me. The problem I ran into is that our spirit is multidimensional and to try to capture it in a flat plane like this illustration makes it inaccurate.

The organs are volatile and move as if they were masses of shiny smoke that enter into and exit from the different spheres of the spiritual world. As you may understand, it would be much easier to capture it on a special effects-video, but despite this, my drawing will help you understand our configuration.

Communion, conscience, mind and heart are the four main components, or organs inside of our spirit. Aside from these, we have systems that help its functioning.

Among these we find the intuition, the seat of power, the inheritance, the spiritual senses, the motion system or wheels of the spirit, and the spiritual garments or dwelling of the spirit.

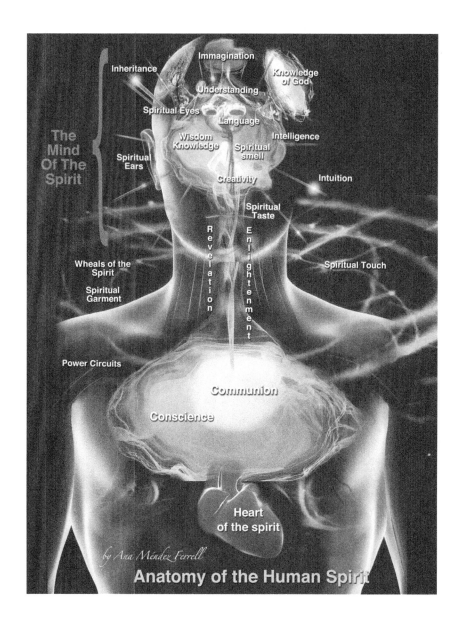

Figure 15 - Anatomy of The Spirit of Man

A. Central Organs of our Spirit

1. Communion

Communion is the central part of our spirit and is located inside the golden bowl. Previously, as we studied it, we saw some of its various functions. This is the part where the Spirit of God is united with the spirit of man. The fountain of life that nourishes the spirit flows from this place. As we can see in the illustration, communion is surrounded by the conscience and is directly connected to the heart of the spirit, and to the mind through spiritual conduits.

The spirit that has been vivified by Christ, and has been born again, has all of its parts connected to the communion organ. Everything that comes to us from God is established in this place first, and then rises up or is projected to other parts of the spirit.

In the case of a recently converted person, God begins the process of awakening the different parts of the spirit that have been dormant because of sin. He will begin to illuminate and awaken every part from this place of communion.

In the case of an unconverted person, the spirit is completely separated from God and is dead, as far as having communion with Him. However, there are other functions that remain alive in all human beings and we will analyze them later on.

2. The Conscience

The conscience is a very sensitive part of our spirit, and it surrounds communion, the heart, and both the spirit and the soul. It is also connected to wisdom and understanding, through spiritual conduits, and to The Fear of The Lord in our inner lampstand. Although sin turned off this candlestick from the time of Adam, our conscience remains mostly activated so we can know right from wrong.

> *For God knows that in the day you eat of it your eyes will be opened, and you will be like God, knowing good and evil."*
>
> *Genesis 3:5*

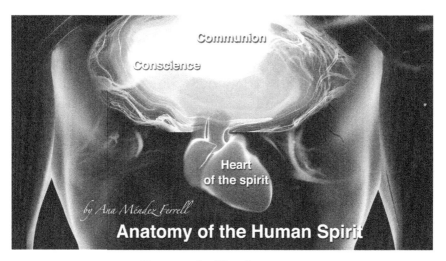

Figure 16 - The Conscience

These are the eyes, that illuminate or give understanding and discernment to our conscience. This is one of the few parts of our spirit that is awake within us, whether we are believers or non-believers. We are all born with the God given ability to discern what is good and what is not.

> *(... for when Gentiles, who do not have the law, by nature do the things in the law, these, although not having the law, are a law to themselves,*

who show the work of the law written in their hearts, their conscience also bearing witness, and between themselves their thoughts accusing or else excusing them)

Romans 2:14-15

When man continuously sins, a hardening of the conscience takes place and causes him to be more and more desensitized to the will of God, thus producing dense vails of cauterization. Having this particular lamp extinguished will inevitably lead to the heart becoming a heart of stone.

To the pure all things are pure, but to those who are defiled and unbelieving nothing is pure; but even their mind and conscience are defiled.

Titus 1:15

speaking lies in hypocrisy, having their own conscience seared with a hot iron,

1 Timothy 4:2

Unbelief, hypocrisy and lies, as these verses show, lead to the hardening of the heart in the part that surrounds it, which is the conscience. This is the condition of the soul, which has taken over, and no longer hears the inner voice that wants to keep him from doing what is wrong.

These hardened veils of the conscience are what are referred to as the foreskin of the heart or being stiff-necked.

Therefore circumcise the foreskin of your heart, and be stiff-necked no longer.

Deuteronomy 10:16

The conscience, being surrounded by the place of communion, is also a door into the knowledge of God and into the understanding of His precepts.

When we convert with our heart, the veil or foreskin is removed, allowing the divine seed to enter and be established in the area of communion. In that moment, the lamp of The Fear of The Lord is ignited and with it, also the rest of the lamps, starting with the central one which is the Spirit of Yahweh or Jehovah.

But even to this day, when Moses is read, a veil lies on their heart.

Nevertheless when one turns to the Lord, the veil is taken away.

Now the Lord is the Spirit; and where the Spirit of the Lord is, there is liberty.

But we all, with unveiled face, beholding as in a mirror the glory of the Lord, are being transformed into the same image from glory to glory, just as by the Spirit of the Lord.

2 Corinthians 3:15-18

When we genuinely receive the Spirit of God in our golden bowl, we are exposed to the light, which transforms us in the measure that we see God's Glory. This way our lamps are lit.

Now we are ready for God to inscribe His laws within us to walk in righteousness, according to His will.

Then I will give them one heart, and I will put a new spirit within them, and take the stony heart out of their flesh, and give them a heart of flesh,

Ezekiel 11:19

This has become a sensitive, flexible and teachable heart that the Father can train and counsel in order to form us as His true children.

I will bless the Lord who has given me counsel; my heart also instructs me in the night seasons.

Psalms 16:7

When the lamp of the "Fear of God" is lit, the lamp of wisdom is also ignited, since both lights work hand in hand.

The fear of the Lord is the beginning of wisdom; a good understanding have all those who do His commandments. ...

Psalms 111:10a

B. The Lamp of the Body

The conscience, which surrounds communion, is what is referred to as the "Lamp of the Body" and it determines the level of light in a person. This is what Jesus was referring to when He talked about our "eyes." He was not talking about our physical eyes; He was talking about a part in our inner being that determines how much light or how much darkness is in us.

> *"The lamp of the body is the eye. If therefore your eye is good, your whole body will be full of light.*
>
> *But if your eye is bad, your whole body will be full of darkness. If therefore the light that is in you is darkness, how great is that darkness!*
>
> *Matthew 6:22-23*

> *And why do you look at the speck in your brother's eye, but do not consider the plank in your own eye?*
>
> *Or how can you say to your brother, 'Let me remove the speck from your eye'; and look, a plank is in your own eye?*
>
> *Hypocrite! First remove the plank from your own eye, and then you will see clearly to remove the speck from your brother's eye.*
>
> *Matthew 7:3-5*

A corrupted conscience, either through sin, unbelief, soul wounds, or religiosity sees everything as bad. His conscience has become a persecutor of others and is cauterized from giving or receiving true love.

To the pure all things are pure, but to those who are defiled and unbelieving nothing is pure; but even their mind and conscience are defiled.

Titus 1:15

C. The Mind of the Spirit

This is one of the most important parts of our spirit, where the majority of our lamps are found.

An awakened spirit grows until the Mind of Christ is totally formed in him. As we said before, everything concerning God, His knowledge, revelation and all of what His thoughts imply, rises into the area of communion towards the spiritual mind.

From this place the designs and hidden treasures of God rise up in the form of revelation or illumination.

1. Love is the Power that awakens the Mind of the Spirit

When we are exercised in the love and the knowledge of God, by faith, He opens up His mysteries and His best kept secrets.

that their hearts may be encouraged, being knit together in love, and attaining to all riches of the full assurance of understanding, to the knowledge of the mystery of God, both of the Father and[a] of Christ, in whom are hidden all the treasures of wisdom and knowledge.

Colossians 2:2-3

117

Knowledge without love leads to vanity and that is why God reserves His most precious jewels for those that truly love. To love does not mean being pleasant and loving with each other or with God himself.

To love means having the same nature as the Father who gave His only son for us. Love is filled with justice, sacrifice, generosity, and denial of ourselves.

Love is the holiness of God manifested, and without love, there is no holiness. The waters of life flow from our spirit to awaken our internal being. Love is the fire that ignites our lamps. It is the light that brings forth the understanding and opens the eyes of the spirit.

The light, that love produces radiates through the conscience, seeing others with grace and favor, just like God saw us.

> *For the love of Christ compels us, because we judge thus: that if One died for all, then all died; and He died for all, that those who live should live no longer for themselves, but for Him who died for them and rose again.*
>
> *Therefore, from now on, we regard no one according to the flesh. Even though we have known Christ according to the flesh, yet now we know Him thus no longer.*
>
> *2 Corinthians 5:14-16*

*that He would grant you, according to the riches of His glory, to be strengthened with might through **His Spirit in the inner man**, that Christ may dwell in your hearts through faith; that you, being rooted and **grounded in love**, may be able to comprehend with all the saints what is the width and length and depth and height— to know the love of Christ which passes knowledge; that you may be **filled with all the fullness of God**.*

Ephesians 3:16-19

To try to receive and understand the mind of Christ without being grounded in all forms and outreach of love, is impossible because this is the fountain of all knowledge.

2. The Different Parts of the Spiritual Mind

In order to make our study more comprehensible, I will separate the different components of the mind into 6 sections:

> a. Organs of Knowledge
>
> b. Creativity
>
> c. Language
>
> d. Spiritual Senses
>
> e. Intuition
>
> f. Inheritance
>
> g. The Seat of God´s Power

a. Organs of Knowledge

I will separate these types of organs in two categories. The first is a group of organs that operate by interacting with one another. This group is composed of the understanding,mscience, intelligence, and wisdom and they are an essential part of the spiritual mind.

The second is the imagination, which serves as an instrument to the first.

1. Understanding, Science, Intelligence and Wisdom

The understanding is the organ that receives light and revelation from the area of communion. It decodes it so that our natural mind can express it in the form of knowledge. Understanding relies on spiritual science, wisdom and intelligence to lead us into "all revealed truth."

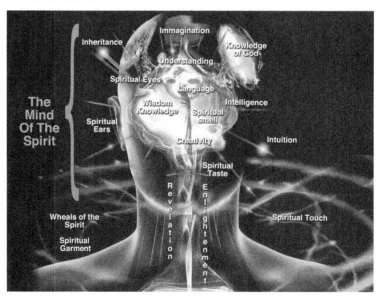

Figure 17 - The Mind of The Spirit and its Components

When we receive a vision, a dream, a Rhema[16] word or a scripture that resonates in our spirit, it rises to the area of understanding to be processed.

For example, in the case of dreams that come from God, there are some that can be complicated due to their symbolism. The interpretation must come from God so that we will not make a mistake.

> *Inasmuch as an excellent spirit, knowledge, understanding, interpreting dreams, solving riddles, and explaining enigmas were found in this Daniel, whom the king named Belteshazzar, now let Daniel be called, and he will give the interpretation.*
>
> *Daniel 5:12*

As we wake up and meditate on the dream, it can be confusing at times, but we know if we persevere in inquiring the interpretation from God, He will give it.

The dream that originated in the area of communion to reveal a mystery or to warn us of something, rises up through the conduits of revelation and enters into the understanding to be interpreted. It is then processed and suddenly, "the light comes on," and we are able to understand what God wanted to say.

The same thing happens with an invention that comes from heaven. At first we vaguely perceive it. We cannot see all of its form and all of its parts with clarity, but when we meditate on it, we capture it completely.

The prophetic gifts of the Spirit of God operate in these areas: word of knowledge, word of wisdom and prophecy.

---

[16] Word revealed directly by God to the spirit of man.

The enemy is extremely interested in veiling this area of our spirit because this is where Christ and His mysteries are revealed to us. When he perceives sin, unbelief or a mental and religious Christianity, he immediately establishes a veil that blinds the understanding.

> *whose minds the god of this age has blinded, who do not believe, lest the light of the gospel of the glory of Christ, who is the image of God, should shine on them.*
>
> *2 Corinthians 4:4*

Many who call themselves Christians have a certain amount of understanding regarding salvation, but they are unable to see Christ in His Glory as the answer to all of their problems here on earth. They live in unbelief because their hearts have never been genuinely converted.

> *But their minds were blinded. For until this day the same veil remains unlifted in the reading of the Old Testament, because the veil is taken away in Christ. But even to this day, when Moses is read, a veil lies on their heart. Nevertheless when one turns to the Lord, the veil is taken away.*
>
> *2 Corinthians 3:14-16*

2. Imagination

The imagination is the visual screen of our spirit. It is directly connected to the area of communion, understanding, and creativity in the spirit. In the soul, it is connected to the mind and the heart. It receives the visual images we perceive in our inner being either from God, from the enemy, or from our flesh.

Those who have a pure heart receive visions and dreams from God. That is where we can see God through the Holy Spirit.

Blessed are the pure in heart, for they shall see God.

Matthew 5:8

A little while longer and the world will see Me no more, but you will see Me. Because I live, you will live also.

John 14:19

A perverse heart and mind will conceive evil imaginations.

The wealth of the rich [is] the city of his strength, and as a wall set on high in his own imagination.

Proverbs 18:11 YLT

And you have done worse than your fathers, for behold, each one follows the dictates of his own evil heart, so that no one listens to Me.

Jeremiah 16:12

As long as a heart is not purified with the knowledge of truth, it will inevitably send corrupted and deceitful images to the imagination.

The saying, "everything is the color of the crystal with which it is seen" clearly applies to the heart, and how it perverts truth based on the images that come from the memory.

A person that has been betrayed will imagine that no one in the world is worthy of his or her trust. Another person, trained in believing in the end of the world, will imagine all sorts of worldwide calamities.

Someone suffering from a trauma will see all kinds of things that terrorize him or her on their spiritual screen.

The imagination is extremely powerful, and because it is linked to the heart and to memory, it exerts a great deal of influence on our will. There are times when God asks something difficult of us, intending to break a certain thought structure or behavior. At that point, the imagination will send images of pain and fear to keep us from taking that step.

For example, God wants us free from medicine, and asks that we stop taking a certain one. Fear, stemming from the fallen soul sends signals to the imagination, and the person begins to fabricate an entire story in their mind about how the body will be destroyed by lack of medication.

The spirit is willing, but the flesh that is weak, takes over the imagination and the will in setting up all kinds of obstacles.

If the spirit overcomes and stands on the Truth, it will send a victorious projection, full of faith to the imagination.

Both accurate and inaccurate Biblical teaching causes people to have visions that have to do with the form of thinking they were indoctrinated with.

Normally, when people are developing their spiritual senses, these will be affected by the way they think or believe.

A person that upholds a certain doctrine will have dreams or visions in relation to that doctrine. One who has never heard of that theory will not see anything related to that.

What I believe is projected in my imagination. Everyone is, has, and receives what they decide to believe.

That is why it is so important to have a personal and direct revelation of Christ in our lives, and not based on someone else's revelation, no matter how great it may seem to us.

I believe it is very important that we understand that our imagination must be completely consecrated to God. We must close all connections to the fallen heart and the corrupted memory.

Later, when we study the doors of the spirit, we will learn how to protect this organ so that it will be used only by the Spirit of God.

The majority of the dreams that come from God, as well as those that have been infiltrated by the devil, full of lies and oppression, are projected on this screen. The screen also receives the dreams that come from our own soul, which is continuously trying to express itself.

b. Creativity

This is one of the parts that are mostly activated when the spirit has awakened, since God is essentially a creator.

While the spirit is in a state of sleep, the soul takes on the creative function. God, in His immense love, has given both believers and non-believers the ability to create and invent great things. When He made us in His image and likeness, He placed extraordinary abilities within us, and many of these remained after the fall, including this one.

The greatest inventor in the universe is God, and throughout the ages He has been revealing science, technology, as well as music and art to man.

Unfortunately, the soul that does not know the Lord will use all of this for a selfish end, to exalt itself, to make great amounts of money and in many cases for plans of evil.

If all technological, scientific and artistic advances were in the hands of the Sons of God, the world would be different, and one day it will be. What is important to understand right now, is that the majority of what man has accomplished has been through people that did not have God as their Lord; now imagine what we could accomplish with a spirit united with the Creator.

Creativity is an unending river of wisdom, intelligence and understanding. It is the fountain out of which all beauty that crowns heaven and earth flows from. It is where we can feel and touch God, where we can immerse ourselves in the wonderful torrents of music and splendor coming out of Him.

It is the heartbeat of life itself that continuously renews and transforms itself, leading us to create a society that is in a constant state of evolution and change. When we stop creating, we begin to die.

That is why monotony, and the rigid, restrictive religious structures and systems of the world begin to kill our spirit. Creativity is our vital essence and it continuously seeks to innovate and invent from the simplest forms, from creating a happy moment, to the infinite quest to conquer all of our dreams.

This is the place where God sends His designs, His inventions and everything that has to do with creating something. It is the laboratory of the spirit and the telescope to search out and penetrate into the most extraordinary experiences with God.

This is the converging point, where various currents of the spirit stem from communion, wisdom and intelligence. From that point, these concepts rise into the imagination and are then processed by understanding.

In order to produce what comes from the heart and the intelligence of God, we must have a clean heart. When we analyze the heart, we will see the tremendous influence it has when it comes to either opening or blocking what comes from our spirit.

When Jesus said, *"Blessed are the pure in heart, for they will see God,"* He was not only referring to the revelation of His image, but to everything He is.

God has honored me with His creativity to paint and create all kinds of printed or cinematographic art. This has led me to meet many graphic artists who have a heart to create for the Kingdom of God and to use their talents for His Glory.

Unfortunately, I have run into a very common problem. Wanting to create for God does not simply mean having a desire to do so and getting started. Creativity must be revealed by God, and it is intimately related to the condition of the heart. The more freedom and purity in the person's soul, the more the torrents of revelation to create will abound. On the other hand, if the soul is not free and pure, conflicts and darkness within the soul will continuously emerge in the works of these artists.

c. Language

This is one of the areas I am most passionate about since my heart overflows with a desire to communicate the Kingdom of God to the nations in their own language.

Language is clear evidence that man does not come from spontaneous creation or that man has evolved from a primate.

We speak and communicate because God is a God that speaks, and has placed within man the ability to express thoughts and feelings through the means of words. Jesus Himself is The Incarnate Word or "The Word" made flesh. Everything was made through "The Word," which brought all things from the invisible to the visible.

And "*GOD SAID…and it was.*"

Language comes from the spirit, and it is in that place that every word that comes out of our mouth flows, whether we are believers or not.

The Miracle of Speaking a Language

When we are born in this world, our spirit, which comes from God is complete, but the soul is in a state of development. Part of it was formed inside our mother's womb and the other is formed through culture and the information we receive. Our parents and the society where we were raised will be important factors in the development of our soul.

During this process, the spirit sends the soul all elements required for storing, decoding and understanding the words we hear.

During the first years of life, our soul is catching and storing all the words that are spoken around us.

The spirit then sends the structure of this language to the soul through revelation. In order to speak, the baby will not have to study grammar or the proper organization of a phrase, or need to know if it is in past tense, subjunctive tense, conditional or any kind of grammatical tense. This is revealed by his spirit.

God has supernaturally given me the ability to speak six languages. I received the majority of them through the Holy Spirit in the blink of an eye, while I preached on a foreign platform.

These miracles caused me to focus my attention on this extraordinary gift, God has given man.

All languages were given to man in a split second during the confusion God sent to the builders of the tower of Babel. This was done to interrupt satan's plans to bring the world into one agreement with him, which has always been his intention[17].

Also, on the Day of Pentecost, God gave the disciples in the upper room, the languages of the world in a split second, so that they could take the Gospel to all nations.

And when this sound occurred, the multitude came together and were confused, because everyone heard them speak in his own language.

Acts 2:6

If we observe, in both cases, languages were given by God in a split second. This tells us that languages are first received in the spirit, and not in the mind. The mind reasons, but the spirit flows. When we speak, we do not stop and think whether we need to place the noun first, then the verb and then the predicate at the end. We simply speak. It is like a river that flows out of us, and that flow can only come from the spirit.

The mind is able to memorize a poem a play or a scripture, and can analyze and determine the best way to write a certain phrase in a book or a brochure. But, that is not what gave us the ability to speak when we were children.

---

[17] And the Lord said, "Indeed the people are one and they all have one language, and this is what they begin to do; now nothing that they propose to do will be withheld from them. 7 Come, let Us go down and there confuse their language, that they may not understand one another's speech. (Genesis 11:6-7)

Now going back to babies, have you ever wondered why a baby who was always spoken to in the second person, as in referring to him as "you," begins to speak in first person saying, "I want …"? How does he know how to conjugate a verb? It is easy for him to associate a certain object with a word, but the miracle is much greater than that.

After the spirit deposits all the words being heard in the storage place for language, it begins to form a structure in the mind where it places all the words. This structure contains grammar, which will aid the baby in putting phrases together, and eventually speaking. Every language has a different structure that must be translated from the spirit to the natural mind.

Generally, in the area of language, the spiritual mind and natural mind are united. This is one of the parts of the spirit that remains active despite the vital parts of the spirit remaining dormant.

Once the words and the structure are in position, the understanding decodes them, revealing their meaning to our natural mind. In that moment, the baby or the person that wants to speak a new language begins to do so.

If your spirit has been awakened by God and you want to speak a foreign language, ask the Holy Spirit for it, believing.

A good exercise for receiving a new language is reading the Bible in the desired language. Choose a verse you know by heart and read it several times in the foreign language, with an open heart. You will be surprised how the understanding begins to decode a word and then another, until you are literally understanding it completely.

It is important to start speaking even if we sometimes make up words or deform them just like a baby does. In order to learn to walk you had to stand up and take your first steps and you did the same thing when you began to speak.

These first words will begin to connect your hearing with your voice and with the understanding. If you only repeat these words in your mind, that structure will not be formed. We must speak.

d. Spiritual Senses

The soul perceives the natural world and its reality through physical senses. In the same way, the spirit perceives the invisible and eternal reality through spiritual senses.

1. Spiritual Eyes

The Bible speaks of several spiritual eyes in our spirit. I only placed one pair of eyes in this illustration since I was limited to designing something multidimensional in plain form, and I wanted to make it more understandable for you.

Eyes of Understanding

The eyes of your understanding being enlightened; that you may know what is the hope of His calling, what are the riches of the glory of His inheritance in the saints,

Ephesians 1:18

God called Paul, and anyone else who calls himself a minister of God, to open the eyes of their understanding, so people will be able to leave darkness and come to the light.

But rise and stand on your feet; for I have appeared to you for this purpose, to make you a minister and a witness of the things, which you have seen ...

To open their eyes, in order to turn them from darkness to light, and from the power of satan to God ...

Acts 26:16a; 18a

These eyes are directly connected to the conscience and the understanding. Their objective is to cause people to clearly see their condition and understand their need for salvation and reconciliation with God. The eyes are opened when people seek God with a sincere, contrite and humble heart. Many people, who apparently follow Christ, still have their eyes closed because their heart has never truly been converted, but rather they just follow a religion. This is what Jesus referred to when He said: seeing they do not see, and hearing they do not hear[18].

Eyes to see into the invisible Dimension

Our spirit was created with eyes capable of seeing in the dimensions of God's Kingdom. These eyes are opened with "the new birth", and are perfected as we exercise them prophetically.

Then he took up his oracle and said: The utterance of Balaam the son of Beor, the utterance of the man whose eyes are opened,

The utterance of him who hears the words of God, who sees the vision of the Almighty, who falls down, with eyes wide open

Numbers 24:3-4

---

[18] Therefore I speak to them in parables, because seeing they do not see, and hearing they do not hear, nor do they understand. (Matthew 13:13)

The Seven Eyes of God within our Spirit

And I looked, and behold, in the midst of the throne and of the four living creatures, and in the midst of the elders, stood a Lamb as though it had been slain, having seven horns and seven eyes, which are the seven Spirits of God sent out into all the earth.

Revelation 5:6

Wherever the seven spirits of God are, so are His eyes, which help us see and understand the ways of God.

2. Spiritual Ears

This is a very important organ because God communicates through it. The ears are found in the back of our spirit, in the nape zone and are connected to the area of communion, to the conscience and to the heart.

Your ears shall hear a word behind you, saying, "This is the way, walk in it," Whenever you turn to the right hand or whenever you turn to the left.

Isaiah 30:21

This is the type of ear Jesus was referring to when He said:

He, who has an ear, let him hear what the Spirit says to the churches.

Revelation 2:29

When the ear is awake, it leads to The Fear of The Lord, as well as seeking of His unfathomable riches and revelation. Faith, which is found within the area of communion, is activated and strengthened when we hear with an open heart.

So then faith comes by hearing, and hearing by the word of God.

Romans 10:17

We will see this in more detail when we study the heart.

3. Spiritual Taste

Very few people have developed this sense. John the Apostle ate the little book given to him by the angel and it was sweet in his mouth and bitter in his stomach[19].

Prophet Ezekiel ate the scroll the Lord gave him and experienced the same thing[20].

My husband Emerson fasts up to 200 or more days per year, and has told me that angels have descended with heavenly food to strengthen him and he describes it as liquid light with a sweet taste.

---

[19] Then I took the little book out of the angel's hand and ate it, and it was as sweet as honey in my mouth. But when I had eaten it, my stomach became bitter. (Revelation 10:10)

[20] And He said to me, "Son of man, feed your belly, and fill your stomach with this scroll that I give you." So I ate, and it was in my mouth like honey in sweetness. (Ezekiel 3:3)

4. Spiritual Smell

God gifted our spirit with the ability to smell in the spiritual world. It is one of the senses frequently developed by those who have the gift of discernment of spirits.

Foul spirits stink just like sin, which carries death. God trains us so that we can identify the spirits.

Those who have come out of strong sexual sin easily identify another person that has been in a similar situation by their smell. The same thing occurs with those who have come out of drugs or the occult.

On the heavenly side, there are wonderful aromas that manifest with the presence of God. Genuine worship that comes from the spirit produces fragrances that are extremely pleasant to God.

Jesus Himself is called the *Rose of Sharon* and the *Lily of the Valley* because of the high frequency contained in the aromatic oils that come from these flowers.

The aroma of these flowers, as well as spikenard, have such an impact on the spiritual realm that even the demons manifest when they smell these oils.

When Mary broke the alabaster jar filled with spikenard perfume, the demons within Judas manifested, and he left that place to betray Jesus.

My husband, an expert in aromas, wrote a book called, "The Breath of God over Essential Oils." In this book, he explains the powerful revelations regarding heavenly aromas and their influence in the spiritual realm.

God is a God that loves and delights in aromas and that is why He determined there would be a special anointing and a ministry of the "perfumer", responsible for the holy fragrances.

This ministry understood the spiritual impact contained in these aromas, as well as the method of mixing them according to the Holy Spirit.

This is not the type of perfume created for us to smell good or to be more attractive to the opposite sex, as we find today in the marketplace.

> *And you shall make from these a holy anointing oil, an ointment compounded according to the art of the perfumer. It shall be a holy anointing oil.*
>
> *Exodus 30:25*

This revelation regarding the aromas of God is very important because it connects us to the fragrances and frequencies of heaven, and it causes our spirit to become more sensitive.

In the same way a true prophetic worshiper hears the sounds of heaven, the perfumer smells the fragrances of heaven. To God, flowers are not the only ones with fragrance; love, obedience, generosity and sacrifice release a fragrant smell in the spiritual world that rises up to God.

> *And walk in love, as Christ also has loved us and given Himself for us, an offering and a sacrifice to God for a sweet-smelling aroma.*
>
> *Ephesians 5:2*
>
> *Indeed I have all and abound. I am full, having received from Epaphroditus the things sent from you, a sweet-smelling aroma, an acceptable sacrifice, well pleasing to God.*
>
> *Philippians 4:18*

5. Spiritual Touch

Our spirit, just like our body is covered with a sort of a spiritual skin, which we will refer to as garments, or spiritual habitation.

It is what shapes our spirit, and that is why after death, we maintain a spiritual physiognomy. Angels as well as demons, being spiritual beings, have a visible form that distinguishes them from one another.

This spiritual garment begins to take the shape of Christ in the measure we grow in Him, as we are transformed into His very image[21].

Paul the Apostle understood the importance of these garments, and he would groan to be clothed in them. They contain the resurrection of Christ, which absorbs all mortality in us.

> *For in this we groan, earnestly desiring to be clothed with our habitation, which is from heaven,*
>
> *if indeed, having been clothed, we shall not be found naked.*
>
> *For we who are in this tent groan, being burdened, not because we want to be unclothed, but further clothed, that mortality may be swallowed up by life.*
>
> *2 Corinthians 5:2-4*

> *But put on the Lord Jesus Christ, and make no provision for the flesh, to fulfill its lusts.*
>
> *Romans 13:14*

---

[21] But we all, with unveiled face, beholding as in a mirror the glory of the Lord, are being transformed into the same image from glory to glory, just as by the Spirit of the Lord.(2 Corinthians 3:18)

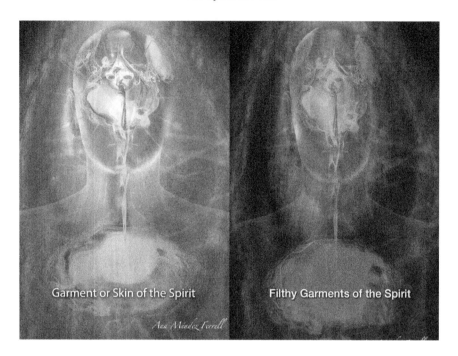

Figure 18 / 19 - Clean / Filthy Garments of the Spirit

These garments determine what is able to penetrate the rest of our being, such as disease, traumatic strokes caused by the iniquity of people that want to hurt us, or attacks from the devil.

> *"For the Lord God of Israel says that He hates divorce, for it covers one's garment with violence (Iniquity)," says the Lord of hosts. "Therefore take heed to your spirit, that you do not deal treacherously."*
>
> *Malachi 2:16*

We observe in this passage how the garments of the spirit are stained with violence or iniquity, making us vulnerable in the spiritual world; that is why the Lord stresses the words: "*Take heed.*"

When we convert to Christ with all of our heart, we are clothed with His grace and this grants us our salvation, if we stay in Him. However, clothing ourselves with the Lord Jesus Christ implies laboring for inner growth.

My little children, for whom I labor in birth again until Christ is formed in you,

Galatians 4:19

Christ is formed in us as an invincible armor. In order for this to take place we must forge within us the righteousness of God through faith, which is our breastplate and shield. We must also exchange our mind for the Mind of Christ, which is our helmet of salvation.

During Israel's captivity in Babylon, God visited Joshua the High Priest. The years of captivity in the midst of pagans had contaminated his spiritual garments, and so they needed to be changed for Israel's restoration to begin. The Lord orders him to remove his old garments and to be clothed with new ones, not because He is interested in an external dress, but because this had to do with what was on the inside.

The garments of the flesh and the fallen soul are filthy rags, and those of the spirit are very elegant rich clothes.

Now Joshua was clothed with filthy garments, and was standing before the Angel.

Then He answered and spoke to those who stood before Him, saying, "Take away the filthy garments from him."

And to him He said, "See, I have removed your iniquity from you, and I will clothe you with rich robes."

And I said, "Let them put a clean turban on his head."

Zechariah 3:3-5

I remember when I converted; the Lord opened my spiritual eyes to see the condition of my soul. It was horrible to see myself through the eyes of God, and to see my garments as disgusting and smelly rags as a result of sin. Seeing myself this way before God's purity, led me to hate evil, and give myself to Him with all my heart.

We sometimes think of ourselves very differently from the way He sees us. Jesus spoke a very significant parable regarding this, and compared the Kingdom of God to a great wedding.

But when the king came in to see the guests, he saw a man there who did not have on a wedding garment.

So he said to him, 'Friend, how did you come in here without a wedding garment?' And he was speechless.

Then the king said to the servants, 'Bind him hand and foot, take him away, and cast him into outer darkness; there will be weeping and gnashing of teeth.

"For many are called, but few are chosen.

Matthew 22:11-14

The sense of spiritual touch is not just about our spiritual garments. We also have the ability to touch and perceive the spiritual world through it.

The presence of angels can be felt by stretching out our hands and feeling with our spiritual touch. If there is an angel, our spirit will feel heat vibrating in the place where he is. The opposite happens when we encounter spirits of death, they manifests as a cold presence.

e. Intuition

This is the spiritual organ that surrounds our spirit, acting as an antenna or spiritual radar. It is active even if our spirit is dormant in the area of communion with God. It can sense a presence, be it angelic, human or demonic.

Have you ever felt like someone is looking at you or following you? That is intuition capturing it.

These antennas are distributed around our entire spirit. Those who are close to the area of understanding will capture things that have to do with knowing something without ever having studied it or heard of it. We simply know something is a certain way, and we cannot explain it with our natural mind.

We can know what someone else is thinking without necessarily hearing word by word.

Jesus understood intuitively what the religious people spoke in their hearts.

But immediately, when Jesus perceived in His spirit that they reasoned thus within themselves, He said to them, "Why do you reason about these things in your hearts?

Mark 2:8

Intuition will perceive things that occurred in a certain place or that are about to happen. That is why certain people have premonitions even if they are not believers.

The kingdom of darkness usurps this part of the spirit to promote fear and to bring destructive prophecies that never came from God.

When people are not aware of how the Kingdom of God and the kingdom of darkness release their respective prophecies, it is very easy to become confused as to where the information came from.

God communicates with man through the area of communion, but the devil infiltrates through intuition.

One thing that is very important to understand is that there is a layer over the earth that serves as an invisible network, where the kingdom of darkness is continuously sending all kinds of messages of destruction. Hurricanes, earthquakes, wars and plans to destroy the world circulate throughout this network.

When a prophet or someone who is developing their prophetic gifts is not aware of this demonic sphere, they can easily hear words of destruction or fear that their intuition senses. They think that since they have a relationship with God, and the message they are receiving is supernatural, it comes from God, but unfortunately that is not the case.

When God wants to communicate a certain judgment through a prophet, He ALWAYS gives a way out, if the people repent.

A prophecy of destruction without a solution comes from darkness, and not from God. God does not want to destroy the world; He wants to fill it with His knowledge, as the waters cover the sea.

For the earth will be filled with the knowledge of the glory of the Lord, as the waters cover the sea.

Habakkuk 2:14

Nowadays, there are millions of people coming into agreement with plans of destruction from the devil because they ignore the functions of their spirit, and the spiritual spheres that control the world.

It is very important that we be cleansed through the Word of God and that we allow its sword to divide our soul from our spirit. As long as this does not take place, we will consider divine or spiritual, something originating in the soul, which makes it carnal.

For the word of God is living and powerful, and sharper than any two-edged sword, piercing even to the division of soul and spirit, and of joints and marrow, and is a discerner of the thoughts and intents of the heart.

Hebrews 4:12

f. Inheritance

This part of the spirit was designed in Adam to receive God's DNA, but it was corrupted due to the fall. Man entered a state of spiritual death and received the seed of the devil. This caused iniquity, stemming from evil, to enter the man's spirit and be passed on from generation to generation to all human beings.

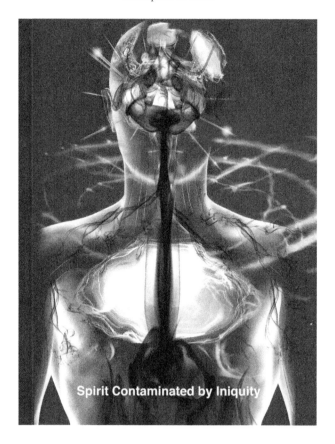

Figure 20 - Anatomy of the Spirit of Iniquity

Our physical body stores all of the information regarding our physical inheritance in the DNA within the cells. It is like a computer's microchip, where all the Data is located. DNA determines whether we are born with our grandfather's eyes, our mother's mouth, our grandmother's hair color or our father's height.

All of this information is physically transmitted from generation to generation. As the cells multiply in the mother's womb, a body begins to be formed according to the design of said information. A similar model is found in the spiritual body.

There is an area that records all spiritual information that is transmitted to our children and subsequent generations and is known as "iniquity".

It is very important to put our attention in cleansing of this area of our spirit, and purge our iniquities to receive God's DNA[22].

Therefore, having these promises, beloved, let us cleanse ourselves from all filthiness of the flesh and spirit, perfecting holiness in the fear of God.

2 Corinthians 7:1

Iniquity comes out of the spirit and is transmitted to the body through the lymphatic system. This is a complex network of narrow vessels, valves, channels, nodules and organs. It resembles a net that goes across the entire body, underneath the skin where energy runs through, and where toxins are contained and is our body's main defense system. Another function is to help protect and maintain the organism's fluids in order.

I will deal with the interconnection between spirit, soul and body thoroughly. We will then see the complete route iniquity takes to install itself in the body's organs and bones.

As he clothed himself with cursing as with his garment, so let it enter his body like water, and like oil into his bones.

Psalms 109:18

---

[22] In my book, "Iniquity," I describe in depth how this exchange can take place.

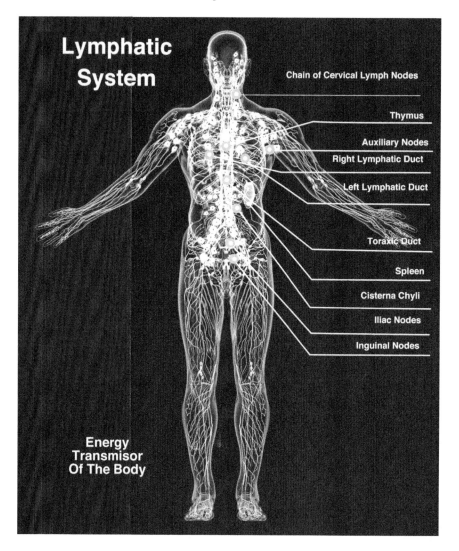

Figure 21 - Lymphatic System

g. The Seat of God's Power

There is an area of our spirit where the power of God dwells, which is one of the seven Spirits of God. This area is directly connected to the one of communion and is where the gifts of miracles, healings and creative wonders of God manifest.

Another way to explain it would be the spiritual engine. Samson by example, received his strength in this part of his spirit. It is also where the blast of power came from the hands of Moses to divide the Red Sea. We see this in the description of God's power coming out of Jesus.

His brightness was like the light; He had rays flashing from His hand, and there His power was hidden.

Habakkuk 3:4

Paul the Apostle also knew this power and he expressed it in the following way.

Now to Him who is able to do exceedingly abundantly above all that we ask or think, according to the power that works in us.

Ephesians 3:20

The apostles had received the Spirit of God when Jesus blew on them before His ascension, however He said:

But you shall receive power when the Holy Spirit has come upon you; and you shall be witnesses to Me in Jerusalem, and in all Judea and Samaria, and to the end of the earth.

Acts 1:8

This tells me that the Holy Spirit can come upon different areas of the spirit and activate them one by one, until we reach His fullness. That is why we see believers with certain parts of their spirit much more developed than others. There are believers who have great intuition or move prophetically, but in the areas of power, they are not very effective. The truth is the gifts of the Spirit come upon different parts of our spirit to develop it in each area[23]

---

[23] Book "Iniquity" by the same author. Pages 34-35

PART III

THE HEART AND SOUL

Chapter 9

THE HEART

The heart is one of the most important parts of our being since it is the center, and the main door to our spirit. It is the organ that determines everything we are, as well as the realization of our destiny on this earth and in eternity.

> *Keep your heart with all diligence, for out of it spring the issues of life.*
>
> *Proverbs 4:23*

The heart determines who we are, how we act and we make all decisions for our lives there.

> *For as he thinks in his heart, so is he.*
>
> *Proverbs 23:7*

Our heart is what causes us to take great steps in life. The strength of our being is concentrated there in order for us to obtain victory, to triumph in tribulations or to take a risk. This is where courage and fear are forged. This is also where a great deal of our health is determined.

A sound heart is life to the body, but envy is rottenness to the bones.

Proverbs 14:30

Most importantly, it is the place where our salvation or condemnation is determined.

For with the heart one believes unto righteousness, and with the mouth confession is made unto salvation.

Romans 10:10

Only the heart is able to lead the soul to true repentance and subdue it in order for us to change our behavior, our intentions and motivations.

The heart is a spiritual bridge, which links our spirit and soul, and is directly connected to the body's cardiac organ.

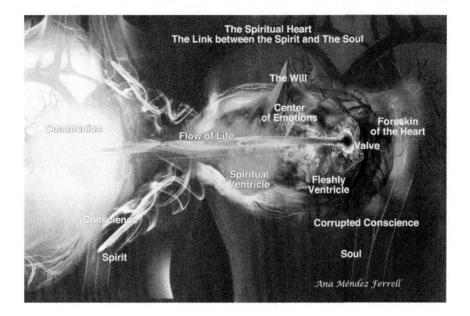

Figure 22 - The Heart, Bridge Between the Spirit and Soul

1. Components of the Heart

In the same way our physical heart has two sides. The spiritual heart is divided in two. One part is connected to the spirit and the other is connected to the soul. The physical heart, which is the image of the spiritual one, receives dirty blood and cellular waste on one side while the other receives the purified blood from the lungs and sends it throughout the body.

a. The Ventricles

This same design is found within our intangible being. We have a carnal ventricle that deals with the issues of the soul, and a spiritual ventricle that receives everything that comes from God and from our spirit.

God writes His laws in the area of the ventricle of the spirit. This part is surrounded by the conscience, which comes from God and was placed within us since birth. Besides it is connected to communion through a conduit that releases the flow of life flows into our entire being.

> *This is the covenant that I will make with them after those days, says the Lord: I will put My laws into their hearts, and in their minds I will write them.*
>
> *Hebrews 10:16*

I have referred to them this way because the heart pumps either iniquity or the power of God and life to our entire being.

The carnal ventricle of the heart is the source of all thoughts that contaminate the soul and the body.

In the spiritual world there are substances. That is why it is written that faith is the substance of things hoped for, and also that iniquity enters the organs and bones to corrupt them with its filthy water and oil.

> *But those things which proceed out of the mouth come from the heart, and they defile a man.*
>
> *Matthew 15:18*

> *As he clothed himself with cursing as with his garment, so let it enter his body like water, and like oil into his bones.*
>
> *Psalms 109:18*

I am poured out like water, and all My bones are out of joint; My heart is like wax; it has melted within Me.

Psalms 22:14

A sound heart is life to the body, but envy is rottenness to the bones.

Proverbs 14:30

b. The Foreskin of the Heart

Surrounding the carnal ventricle we find the foreskin of the heart, which is seen as a dark substance. This is a part of our conscience that thickens and become insensitive due to sin, evil and unbelief; all characteristics of the Adamic nature.

As long as this is not removed and changed through a reformed conscience, it will serve as a cap that will prevent the flow of God from illuminating and irrigating our soul. That is why God calls us to circumcise our hearts, so that His life and holiness can be manifested renovating our souls.

Therefore circumcise the foreskin of your heart, and be stiff-necked no longer.

Deuteronomy 10:16

Later on I will discuss the hardening of the heart and describe how it turns to stone.

The conscience, which surrounds the heart, corrupts and produces unbelief. Corruption not only comes from sin, iniquity or rebellion - a broken and wounded heart becomes corrupted as well. Destructive emotions such as envy, jealousy, bitterness, et cetera are important factors that corrupt the heart. The more corruption there is, the greater the unbelief and the lack of faith.

This foreskin, in the conscience, truly is like a dark lens, which cause the person to see everything distorted. It causes us to distrust everyone and everything. A heart in this condition is blocked in many ways and is not even able to trust God. Their mouth may say they love Him and believe in Him, but their acts and the fruit in their lives show they only trust in themselves and their own reasoning.

> *To the pure all things are pure, but to those who are defiled and unbelieving nothing is pure; but even their mind and conscience are defiled.*
>
> *Titus 1:15*

This corruption forms dense veils that prevent people from seeing God. We were created to see and enjoy our Maker. Jesus is the image of the invisible God and when we have a true conversion, with all of our heart, He manifests and allows us to see Him.

> *But even to this day, when Moses is read, a veil lies on their heart.*
>
> *Nevertheless when one turns to the Lord, the veil is taken away.*

Now the Lord is the Spirit; and where the Spirit of the Lord is, there is liberty.

But we all, with unveiled face, beholding as in a mirror the glory of the Lord, are being transformed into the same image from glory to glory, just as by the Spirit of the Lord.

2 Corinthians 3:15-18

Do you realize what is taking place? When the veil is removed, the Spirit of God comes to us and gives us the freedom to see Him with an unveiled face so that we can be transformed into His image.

c. The Center of Emotions

One of the most relevant parts of the heart is "the center of emotions". Everything we feel, whether good or bad is processed and emanates from the heart.

For from within, out of the heart of men, proceed evil thoughts, adulteries, fornications, murders,

Mark 7:21

The heart is a chest full of treasures, memories, and good and bad experiences. It is the book written about everything we have accumulated in our soul. It is the movie library where all of our experiences are registered and stored. Our personality, as well as our way of thinking and believing is formed there.

A good man out of the good treasure of his heart brings forth good; and an evil man out of the evil treasure of his heart brings forth evil. For out of the abundance of the heart his mouth speaks.

Luke 6:45

Emotions are linked to the two ventricles, the spiritual and the natural. That way, it is capable of processing the feelings that come from the soul, as well as those that come from God, such as joy, peace, or the expectation of a miracle.

Our emotional center is also connected to the physical heart, mind and brain. Therefore, our emotions play a very significant role in our body's chemistry. Joy and happiness, for example, send a signal to the brain and will tell it to release substances called peptides, which then spread into the entire body. These substances are vital for the proper functioning of our organs.

On the other hand, emotions such as sadness, envy or anger to mention just a few, will send negative signals to the brain, and it will supply negative substances, harmful to our health. That is why Scripture states that these types of feelings dry the bones.

A merry heart does good, like medicine, but a broken spirit dries the bones.

Proverbs 17:22

Do not be wise in your own eyes; fear the Lord and depart from evil.

It will be health to your flesh, and strength to your bones.

Proverbs 3:7-8

For my life is spent with grief, and my years with sighing;
My strength fails because of my iniquity, and my bones
waste away.

Psalms 31:10

When I kept silent, my bones grew old through my
groaning all the day long.

Psalms 32:3

Our center of emotions is one of the main doors to the spirit, and is also connected to the nervous, endocrine and glandular systems. Later on I will deal with this topic in more detail. In the meantime, I want to emphasize the conduit where the life of the Spirit flows out of and into the rest of our being. It is found in this part of the heart.

d. The Flow of Life and the Heart Valve

Life flows from our spirit, since our spirit comes from God and is part of Him.

Whether we have received the regeneration of our spirit through Jesus Christ or not, we all received our natural life from God.

When someone is still under the Adamic nature, that person continues to receive the flow of life from his or her spirit in order to exist on this planet.

When someone is full of the Spirit of God, the flow of life will be an abundant stream of resurrection life, springing forth from the center of communion to the rest of his or her being.

The impartation of every perfect gift and divine nature essentially flows from a conduit, which links the spirit to the carnal ventricle (see Figure 22). At the end of it there is a valve that opens and closes as we have intimacy with God.

As long as our hearts have not been circumcised, the valve will remain shut most of the time, allowing a minimum amount of the flow of life necessary to keep the body from dying.

One of the most important functions of this valve is that it is the door through which we can see the invisible Kingdom of God.

As we are born again, we learn that when "we are in the spirit," this valve opens and we are able to see the dimensions in heaven. As we exercise our faith and our expectation to see in the spirit world, the valve expands, allowing our spirit to peek into the invisible realm. (Figure 23)

I was in the Spirit on the Lord's Day, and I heard behind me a loud voice, as of a trumpet,

…

Then I turned to see the voice that spoke with me. And having turned I saw seven golden lampstands,

Revelation 1:10; 12

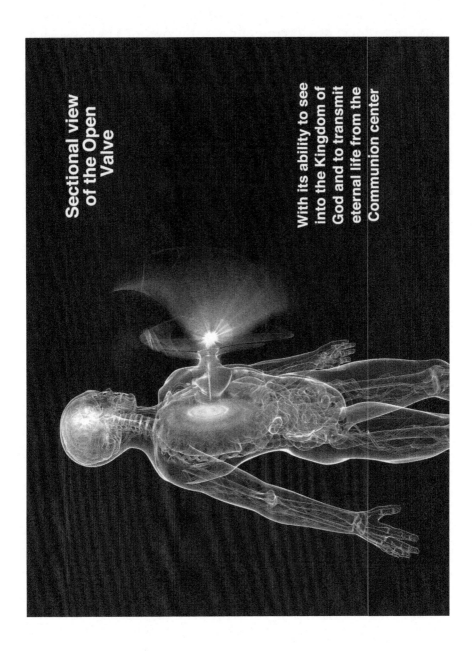

Figure 23 - The Valve of The Spirit

The other way the valve opens up is through love. When my heart is projected towards God to pour out my love for Him, the valve expands and I am able to contemplate His beauty and see Him with an unveiled face.

One thing I have desired of the Lord, that will I seek:

That I may dwell in the house of the Lord all the days of my life, to behold the beauty of the Lord, and to inquire in His temple.

Psalms 27:4

When I meditate on Him from deep within my spirit, I am able to contemplate His Glory and His face.

I will meditate on the glorious splendor of Your majesty, and on Your wondrous works.

Psalms 145:5

Both the channel of life, and the valve, are interconnected with the blood, so the life that comes out from spirit can irrigate the body.

I do not want to give a complicated description of the interconnections between the flow of life and the entire tripartite being, because it would be too much information. The most important thing I want you to understand right now is that the heart, in its three manifestations in spirit, soul and body, is the center of life.

e. The Will

This part of our heart is also connected to the two ventricles, and it is what determines whether we live guided by the Spirit or by the flesh.

Just like the rest of the heart, the will is surrounded by the conscience, which will help us make good or bad decisions.

What is important about this part is that our eternal life, whether in salvation or condemnation depends on it.

For those who live according to the flesh set their minds on the things of the flesh, but those who live according to the Spirit, the things of the Spirit.

For to be carnally minded is death, but to be spiritually minded is life and peace.

...

For if you live according to the flesh you will die; but if by the Spirit you put to death the deeds of the body, you will live.

For as many as are led by the Spirit of God, these are Sons of God.

Romans 8:5-6; 13-14

The will serves as a lever that causes the heart to tilt towards the flesh or towards God.

This is what we refer to as free will. It is free because no one but us can handle it or control it. God cannot make decisions for us, and of course, neither can the devil.

The only thing the devil can do is seduce the will so that the person gives in to his temptations and lies.

As long as the life of a person is not settled in Christ, sin dominates his being. Darkness has established itself in the golden bowl, while the conscience has become almost seared. In this state, the fallen soul hardly listens to the voice of his conscience but loudly hears the seductive lies of the devil.

With the wages of sin being death, "sheol," or "the grave" has great power over the soul that has not been regenerated.

> *Like sheep they are laid in the grave; death shall feed on them; The upright shall have dominion over them in the morning; and their beauty shall be consumed in the grave, far from their dwelling.*
>
> *But God will redeem my soul from the power of the grave, for He shall receive me.*
>
> *Psalms 49:14-15*

This psalm is very revealing and speaks of the influence and the power of death, through sin and deceit.

Despite the fact that the will belongs to us, and only to us, it does receive voices from the realms of life and death, and needs to choose which to hear.

God, in His immeasurable love towards man, is always releasing messages of life and love in our hearts, even among those that do not know Christ. Some times we read in the Bible that God hardens the heart, this happens when the Lord decides to be silent in order to fulfill a certain purpose; at that point the voice of death becomes stronger.

But the Lord hardened Pharaoh's heart, and he did not let the children of Israel go.

Exodus 10:20

In this case, Pharaoh was already under the judgment of God and his evil heart was exposed, so God would be glorified over Israel in a mighty way.

Then I will harden Pharaoh's heart, so that he will pursue them; and I will gain honor over Pharaoh and over all his army, that the Egyptians may know that I am the Lord." And they did so.

Exodus 14:4

When we understand the power God grants us, even while we are still in sin, to have authority over our will, we will subdue it completely.

The heart inclines towards one side or the other through our will. It is as if we play with a balloon full of water, which we can lean one way or the other.

"Now therefore," he said, "put away the foreign gods which are among you, and incline your heart to the Lord God of Israel."

Joshua 24:23

When fear, desperation, sadness, unbelief or sin raises its voice inside our heart, we can always push the lever towards God. In that moment we can take authority and determine that faith, peace, happiness and holiness will take control of the situation.

2. States of the Heart

A. The Heart in a State of Corruption

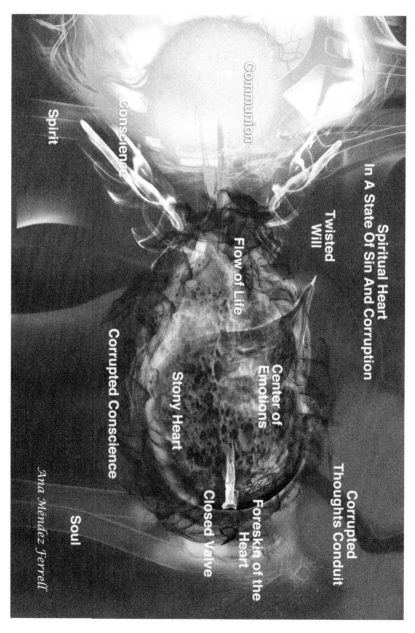

Figure 24 - The Heart in a State of Corruption

As I stated, the heart is the bridge between the spirit and the soul and it can therefore allow or block the flow of life coming from the Spirit.

Sin and corruption of the conscience are the result of the will surrendering to the desires of the flesh. The will that continuously makes decisions based on the flesh is twisted, and tilt towards the soulish heart.

Every time we choose not to believe God, our will yields towards the tree of the knowledge of good and evil.

This is what happened to Adam. He chose the suggestion of the serpent instead of obeying the commandment of God. From that moment on, the tree of human knowledge has a very loud voice, which resonates in the heart, so that we will not believe God.

It is written that anything that does not come from faith is sin. That is because it originates in an unbelieving and corrupted heart that is captive under the realm of sin, which is the "good and evil of this world,"

But he who doubts is condemned if he eats, because he does not eat from faith; for whatever is not from faith is sin.

Romans 14:23

But the Scripture has confined all under sin that the promise by faith in Jesus Christ might be given to those who believe.

Galatians 3:22

Moving in the natural without the use of faith hardens the heart turning it like stone. This is the state of the fallen soul that cannot perceive the things of the Spirit.

As we can see in the illustration (Figure 24), the blackened conscience surrounds the heart, causing it to be insensitive to the voice of God. That is why the flow of life is restrained and reduced to the minimum, while the valve practically remains shut.

In this state the carnal ventricle has taken dominion over the spiritual one and has subjugated it.

The mind that is under the control of the fallen soul receives thoughts of evil, anger, fear, religiosity, unbelief and everything else produced by the corrupted heart.

Many times God will use a difficult circumstance where the heart breaks, and the person cries out to Him, to begin to soften the heart and prepare it to have an encounter with Jesus. Once the heart is sensitized, the conscience will begin to speak and bring the person to repentance. This is the moment the Lord had been waiting for, to knock on the door of the heart and bring the person to His feet. When the person has opened himself to believe, the valve expands enough so that the life of Jesus can penetrate to the depths of the spirit.

B. A Heart after God

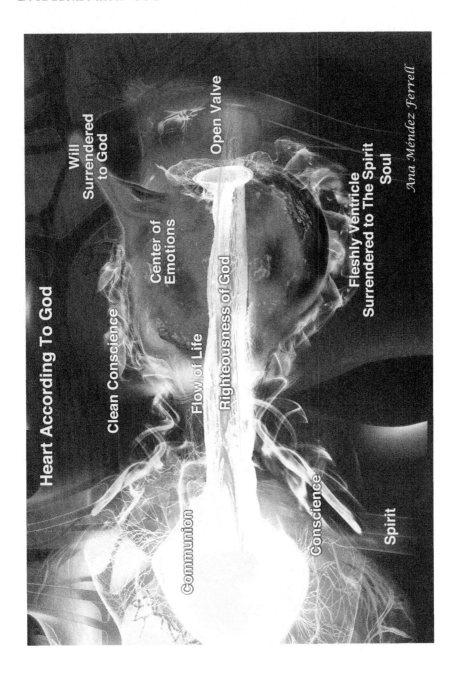

Figure 25 - A Heart after God

This is the heart of those who love and fear God and do not base their lives in the flesh but in the Spirit.

As we can see in the illustration (Figure 25), the will begins to lean towards God, and the spiritual ventricle subdues the carnal one. The life of Christ flows freely through the heart that is surrendered to Him, putting to death the deeds of the flesh.

The opened valve transmits resurrection life to the physical heart and to the blood stream, healing and awaking the mortal body.

*But if the Spirit of Him who raised Jesus from the dead dwells in you, He who raised **Christ from the dead will also give life to your mortal bodies through His Spirit who dwells in you.***

Therefore, brethren, we are debtors - not to the flesh, to live according to the flesh.

For if you live according to the flesh you will die; but if by the Spirit you put to death the deeds of the body, you will live.

For as many as are led by the Spirit of God, these are Sons of God.

Romans 8:11-14

The Spirit of God has taken control and our conscience has been cleansed and restored, making us sensitive to the ways of God and to the realm of the Spirit.

Blessed are the pure of heart for they shall see God.

Matthew 5:8

The heart is now totally working with the spirit and can receive God's thoughts, the revelations and all the secret mysteries. Rivers of living waters and divine knowledge will now flow from the mouths of the believer.

As the heart receives directions directly from our spirit, it will send them to the mind so that we may know God's will in all situations.

> *... since the day we heard it, do not cease to pray for you, and to ask that you may be filled with the knowledge of His will in all wisdom and spiritual understanding;*
>
> *Colossians 1:9b*

3. Dwellings of the Heart

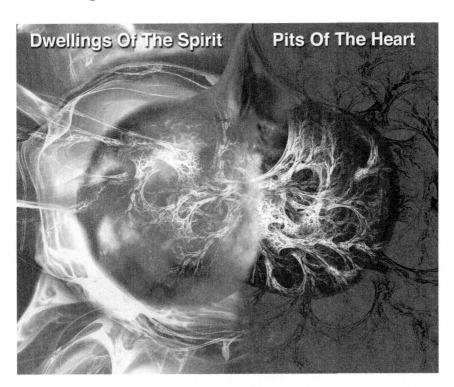

Figure 26 - Internal Dwellings in both Ventricles

a. Dwellings of Glory

The heart has habitations in both of its ventricles and God will use the spiritual ventricle to fill them with wisdom, creativity and faith.

The heart, being the most important door to see and enter the Kingdom of God, is configured with walls and bulwarks to protect God´s presence within the spirit.

The Doors and the Library of Wisdom

In the doors of the Spirit, right in front of the valve, God establishes two powerful doormen, called Wisdom and The Fear of The Lord.

Once the doors have been secured, Wisdom establishes its chambers within the spiritual heart. This is the place where designs, creative inventions, and wisdom, which God gives to those who love Him, are established.

Here we have a very interesting process to observe. The spirit receives all things from God and then transmits them to the heart, which in unison with the renewed mind, execute the will of God.

> *But as it is written: "Eye has not seen, nor ear heard, nor have entered into the heart of man the things which God has prepared for those who love Him."*
>
> *1 Corinthians 2:9*

The first man ever mention filled with the Spirit of God, was named Bezaleel. He and other wise men were given the task of creating all artwork in the Tabernacle of Moses.

"See, I have called by name Bezaleel the son of Uri, the son of Hur, of the tribe of Judah.

And I have filled him with the Spirit of God, in wisdom, in understanding, in knowledge, and in all manner of workmanship, to design artistic works, to work in gold, in silver, in bronze,

in cutting jewels for setting, in carving wood, and to work in all manner of workmanship.

"And I, indeed I, have appointed with him Aholiab the son of Ahisamach, of the tribe of Dan; and I have put wisdom in the hearts of all the gifted artisans, that they may make all that I have commanded you:

Exodus 31:2-6

Here, we see another dwelling place of the heart, which are the chambers of encouragement and happiness.

Dwellings of Encouragement

This is where happiness, courage and generosity are developed. This area is greatly attacked by darkness since these attributes of the heart produce victorious Sons of God in all things.

Be strong and of good courage, do not fear nor be afraid of them; for the Lord your God, He is the One who goes with you. He will not leave you nor forsake you.

Deuteronomy 31:6

A merry heart makes a cheerful countenance, but by sorrow of the heart the spirit is broken.

Proverbs 15:13

Take from among you an offering to the Lord. Whoever is of a willing heart, let him bring it as an offering to the Lord: gold, silver, and bronze;

Exodus 35:5

Meditation Chambers

Be angry, and do not sin. Meditate within your heart on your bed, and be still.

Psalms 4:4

Therefore know this day, and consider it in your heart, that the Lord Himself is God in heaven above and on the earth beneath; there is no other.

Deuteronomy 4:39

Dwellings of Trust and Sincerity

This is the dwelling place where we know in our hearts whether we can trust God or someone else.

These things I have spoken to you, that in Me you may have peace. In the world you will have tribulation; but be of good cheer, I have overcome the world.

John 16:33

Let us draw near with a true heart in full assurance of faith, having our hearts sprinkled from an evil conscience and our bodies washed with pure water.

Hebrews 10:22

Dwellings of Love

Now the purpose of the commandment is love from a pure heart, from a good conscience, and from sincere faith,

1 Timothy 1:5

b. Wells of the Soul

When the heart is broken, wells are created within this ventricle of the soul. These can become deep caverns of fear, desperation, discouragement, sadness, resentment, bitterness and so on - an unending list.

When the Samaritan woman told Jesus he did not have anything to draw out the water from the deep well, it was an analogy to these places in her soul. Having had five husbands, and a sixth being just a lover, we can tell her heart was fragmented in many pieces. The problem of captivity of the soul begins in the heart. These wells are the doors the enemy penetrates to take the fragments of the soul captive.

The heart has been pierced, and deep pits with dark caves are created that connect with our traumatic memory. The soul freezes in the past and continually goes back to the moments that broke it in pieces.

Indeed my belly is like wine that has no vent; it is ready to burst like new wineskins.

Job 32:19

Many times these fragments are taken to regions of captivity where the soul is terribly afflicted and tormented. (**I recommend reading my book, Regions of Captivity where I deal with this topic in great detail.**)

The heart is corrupted in these wells and adopts behaviors, which are harmful to the person and to others. Let take a look at some of them.

Fear

Where can we go up? Our brethren have discouraged our hearts, saying, "The people are greater and taller than we; the cities are great and fortified up to heaven; moreover we have seen the sons of the Anakim there.

Deuteronomy 1:28

And he shall say to them, 'Hear, O Israel: Today you are on the verge of battle with your enemies. Do not let your heart faint, do not be afraid, and do not tremble or be terrified because of them;

Deuteronomy 20:3

Stinginess and Greed

You shall surely give to him, and your heart should not be grieved when you give to him, because for this thing the Lord your God will bless you in all your works and in all to which you put your hand.

Deuteronomy 15:10

Yet your eyes and your heart are for nothing but your covetousness, for shedding innocent blood, and practicing oppression and violence.

Jeremiah 22:17

Bitterness

Thus my heart was grieved, and I was vexed in my mind.

Psalms 73:21

The heart knows its own bitterness, and a stranger does not share its joy

Proverbs 14:10

Your ways and your doings gave procured these things for you. This is your wickedness, because it is bitter, because it reaches to your heart.

Jeremiah 4:18

c. Evil Plots

*No, in heart you work wickedness; you **weigh out** the violence of your hands in the earth.*

Psalms 58:2

Instability and Wandering in the Heart

Therefore I was angry with that generation, and said, 'they always go astray in their heart, and they have not known My ways.

Hebrews 3:10

Contention, Jealousy and Envy

But if you have bitter envy and self-seeking in your hearts, do not boast and lie against the truth. This wisdom does not descend from above, but is earthly, sensual, and demonic.

James 3:14-15

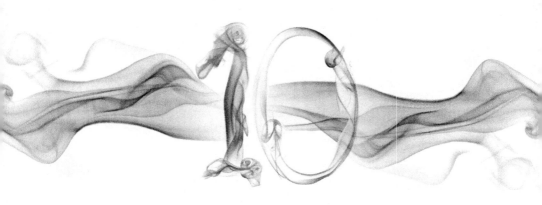

Chapter 10

THE SOUL

As we saw in the beginning, the soul is the decoder between the spirit and the body. Just like the spirit, the soul is composed of a spiritual substance and has all the necessary elements to survive and function, even when the spirit is dormant.

1. States of the Soul

A. The Adamic Soul

From the moment of conception, our spirit, coming out from God, enters our mother's womb, and as it comes into contact with the blood it receives the iniquity of our ancestors. The spirit of the baby that is about to be born, will already be dormant with traits of death.

It is the spirit, that shapes the soul or decoder. What the spirit is, the soul will be. Since the spirit is already deformed because of iniquity, it will create a twisted soul.

The problems, pain, and traumas suffered by the mother will also be transferred to the fetus during gestation, which will continue molding the soul.

The wicked are estranged from the womb; they go astray as soon as they are born, speaking lies.

Psalms 58:3

Behold, I was brought forth in iniquity, and in sin my mother conceived me.

Psalms 51:5

When the infant is born, the undeveloped soul, already in a state of perversion, will start to take dominion over the spirit until it gets full control. This can only be changed when that person consciously converts to the Lord.

In the first years of life, the baby greatly perceives the spiritual world since the spirit is complete, and the soul is still being formed. The spirit has just come from the heart of God and is very sensitive to Him.

Many of the skills of the mind, are not yet fully developed in the baby, such as the ability to choose, the center of emotions as well as behavior structures. During this process, the parents, the environment, social conditions and culture will play a radical role in the shaping of the soul.

When parents do not know how to form the child according to the designs of the Spirit of God, they will shape the tiny soul with all kinds of limiting structures. They will bind it with cultural molds, ways of thinking, fears and manipulations. The result will be a soul completely inadequate to discern and to relate to its spirit. Little by little, as the child develops, he will start to lose innocence with which he felt and spoke to his Heavenly Father.

The soul has taken control, learning the twisted ways of the flesh, and of this world's principles.

His reality will stop being supernatural and he will begin to see the world with its laws and limitations as the true reality of his existence. The malformation will continue to increase in the measure the child begins to practice his own sin, behavior and habits.

Figure 27 - A deformed Soul

As the soul takes on a structure different from the spirit, there will be true enmity between the two. It becomes incapable of operating in the ways and designs of God. If we compare this latest illustration, with the anatomy of the spirit, we will see one has nothing to do with the other. Religion tries to adorn this monstrosity with biblical scriptures, but it is impossible for this to be in agreement with God.

> *But the natural man does not receive the things of the Spirit of God, for they are foolishness to him; nor can he know them, because they are spiritually discerned.*
>
> *1 Corinthians 2:14*

> *Because the carnal mind is enmity against God; for it is not subject to the law of God, nor indeed can be.*
>
> *Romans 8:7*

> *Adulterers and adulteresses! Do you not know that friendship with the world is enmity with God? Whoever therefore wants to be a friend of the world makes himself an enemy of God.*
>
> *James 4:4*

This enmity clearly speaks of the constant clash between the two natures, and how it is impossible to reconcile one with the other.

In the previous illustration, as well as in the following one, we see the soul that has not been regenerated. Thoughts are completely deformed and the memory is full of traumas. The imagination has been filled with lust and twisted images of its identity and the purposes it wants to achieve.

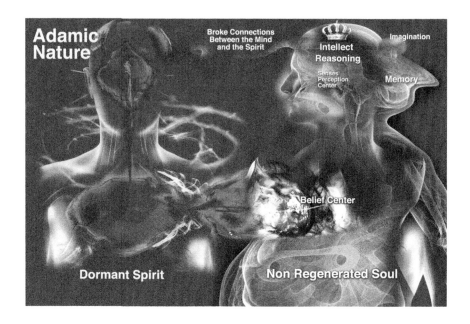

Figure 28 - The Soul That Has Not Been Regenerated

and the Dormant Spirit

The soul has a belly that craves for all kinds of harmful desires to be satisfied. Sexuality has turned into a powerful controller of emotions and reasoning. Intellect and reasoning have become the rulers, along with the emotions and will, as a byproduct of a hardened and seared heart.

Our beliefs come no longer from the voice of God, but from the reasoning of a twisted, afflicted, and corrupt heart.

The Perception of reality is focused only on what the physical senses identify, and is twisted by a mind inclined to fantasy and the lies from the occult.

In the Adamic state, the mind cannot perceive things that come from God, nor can it understand them. The connections between the mind of the soul and the spirit have been broken.

This is why religion, which cannot perceive the things of the Spirit, exalts the knowledge of the soul, trying to put God's wisdom and supernatural nature in a vessel that is unable to understand Him or perceive His ways.

We all come from a fallen and deeply religious nature because Adam believed the lie that he could be like God, and this deceit is continually chasing us. The fallen man feels the need to prove to himself that he can be that god, capable of solving all his problems. The atheist and the free thinker crown is the reasoning of a totally deformed soul. The religious man thinks he can apply some "holiness polish" to that inner monster he has created. He wants to adapt his deformed soul to God, as he fills himself with man-made formulas and commandments.

The truth is God cannot use a soul in that state of deformity. This is the condition of the soul who longs for a savior out of guilt, but will not yield to the Lordship of Christ. The truth is way inside his heart he does not trust God enough to surrender the governing of his life.

The spirit is quickened and awakened when we truly take the soul to the cross, to yield to the supreme King to lead our lives and to enter His Kingdom.

The Adamic nature is incompatible with God's nature. There has never been and never will be a solution in the flesh. The only answer and solution for a fallen and deformed soul is to take it to its death, on the cross of Christso the Spirit of God can form a new creature. A new soul with a new decoder must be created with the ability to translate the designs and thoughts of God, and understand the mysteries of wisdom and understanding.

When the soul is in control and governs someone's life, death is its shepherd. It is sunken in caverns and labyrinths where the enemy traps it and enslaves it.

> *In as much then as the children have partaken of flesh and blood, He Himself likewise shared in the same, that through death He might destroy him who had the power of death, that is, the devil,*
>
> *Hebrews 2:14*

Death is a kingdom with a king, the shepherd to the fallen or carnal souls. It is the voice that leads to the source and depths of death, and causes the souls to trip and fall. His power over those who listen to his voice is fear and slavery.

Figure 29 - The Government of Death within the fallen Soul

And release those who through fear of death were all their lifetime subject to bondage.

Hebrews 2:15

Nevertheless man, though in honor, does not remain;
He is like the beasts that perish.
This is the way of those who are foolish,
And of their posterity who approve their sayings.
Like sheep they are laid in the grave;
Death shall feed on them;

Psalms 49:12-14a

If we understand these things, it will be very clear to us that following Christ and entering into His redemption and His Kingdom requires deep repentance. Whether we take a very powerful step or enter into a quick process, we must genuinely and radically take our soul to death, nailing it to the cross of Christ.

Unending and religious processes that many find themselves in are simply excuses and unbelief, to continue governing their own life. This takes place because they don't realize that death is what truly has them captive and its plan is to lead them to perdition.

Life, death and our eternal destiny are not a game. It is a spiritual reality that deserves all our attention and should be a priority.

Jesus paid the ultimate price to give us an overabundant life, and the true madness and folly is to not dip into these riches.

B. The Renewed Soul

When we finally make the decision to die to our flesh through the Spirit, our regeneration will begin.

In the same way as in our mother's womb, the spirit produced the soul. Now our vivified spirit will create for itself a new soul.

Once we have surrendered our will and lordship to Christ, the process begins.

The spirit will produce an abundant stream of life that will transform the heart, its decisions and will form a renewed mind. The connections of the spirit and the soul will be formed once again so the redeemed mind of our soul will be able to decode and understand what proceeds from the dimension of the Spirit.

Now the seven spirits of God will make their dwelling in the spirit and will quicken it. They will send all revelation, understanding, wisdom, intelligence, and counsel of God to the natural mind.

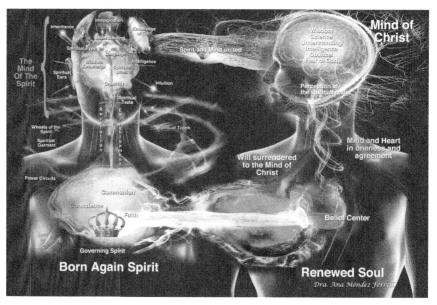

Figure 30 - A Regenerated Soul United with the Reborn Spirit

The mind and the heart of the new creature (soul) will unite in order to produce the power of God and creative miracles.

This takes place because the center of beliefs is now in the place it was created to be, within the spirit, where the faith of God is found.

Faith is the power that makes all things possible. The first thing the Spirit of God will do is uniting the mind and the heart so that faith can manifest the wonders of God.

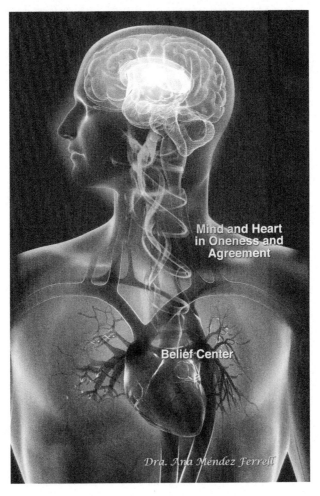

Figure 31 - United Heart and Mind

As long as the mind and heart are not in agreement, the things that proceed from the invisible dimension will be hindered.

Imagine an automobile. God is the energy or the fuel it needs to move wherever the driver wants to go.

The body of the car is the mind. That is where we are convinced that God is powerful and real, to do everything He said He would do. The heart is the engine that makes it run. If the heart doubts, the car does not go anywhere. However, if the heart and the mind come into agreement, they will go where they want to go.

Once the mind is renewed through the impartation of the spirit, it will believe that the spiritual world is the true reality that governs his life. He will enter into dimensions that have no limits, to grow from Glory to Glory, seeing the powerful work of God manifesting in his life.

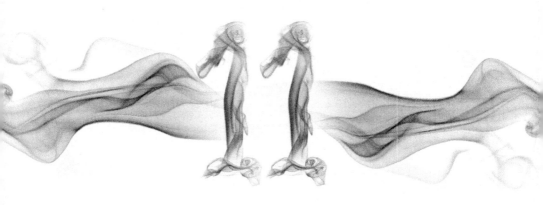

Chapter 11

FREQUENCIES OF THE SPIRIT AND THE SOUL

All things in the universe whether visible or invisible, are formed from energy; both spiritual and physical. Energy forms an electromagnetic field around all things in both realms.

Science measures this energy in terms of frequency. They have not figured out how to define the spiritual dimensions, but they have been able to identify them by the frequency they emit.

The number of repetitive waves in a given amount of time determines a frequency. This can be observed on a screen as vibrations, either long or short, depending on the speed they vibrate.

The spiritual world becomes perceivable and then visible as the frequency increases. The entire Kingdom of God, its angels and its dimensions are vibrating at very high frequencies, which our natural eyes are unable to perceive.

Let us look at the propellers of a helicopter or the blades of a fan, for example. As long as they are still, or are rotating slowly, we are able to see them, but as they accelerate, they become invisible. Now, if we could increase our frequency to that of the fan, we would be able to see the blades again.

This is what happens spiritually when someone is taken up to the heavenly dimensions. This is what Prophet Elijah experienced when he was transported from one place to another. It was also what Paul the Apostle lived when he was taken to the third heaven and to paradise.

> *I know a man in Christ who fourteen years ago—whether in the body I do not know, or whether out of the body I do not know, God knows—such a one was caught up to the third heaven.*
>
> *And I know such a man—whether in the body or out of the body I do not know, God knows how*
>
> *he was caught up into Paradise and heard inexpressible words, which it is not lawful for a man to utter.*
>
> *2 Corinthians 12:2-4*

While it is rather complicated for the body to reach the velocity of the frequencies of heaven, it is much easier for a born again or regenerated spirit.

Now, the kingdom of darkness, the world and the flesh also move through frequencies. Their frequencies are low and slow.

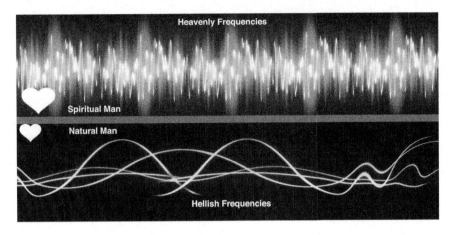

Figure 32 - Heavenly and Hellish Frequencies

When we feel the presence of God, our spirit tends to feel light. It is often felt as if we are ascending or floating on the air. The reason is, the spirit is accelerating its vibration to tune in with heaven. We also feel this when we love intensely and we feel as if we are floating on a cloud of happiness. Also when we worship or exercise our faith strongly. The more intense the experience is, the higher the frequency.

When we studied the wheels of the spirit, we saw how they have the ability to increase their speed and take us to extraordinary experiences.

Now, a soul that has been around low frequencies all of its life due to its fallen condition, wants to remain there. It is its habitat, what it knows and is familiar with. That is why it will do the unthinkable to bring down, and lower the frequency of everything it hears, making it rational, which is the realm of its security. Disgracefully, the lack of understanding regarding how spiritual spheres move, has caused even the interpretation and practicing of the Bible to be affected by these low frequencies.

As spiritual beings we produce fruit, which comes from one frequency or another. When we speak of and project the life of the Lord Jesus through our spirit, we produce the fruit of the spirit. On the contrary, if we were to say something beautiful or religious, even if it is the Word of God, but it is done from the soul, it does not produce anything that remains, yet it can still bring condemnation or affliction.

When the Bible speaks about living in the Spirit, it refers to elevating our soul to the frequencies of light, life, joy, justice and peace.

When the soul remains in low frequencies, it becomes exhausted, afflicted, desperate and fearful, etc. because it is being over taken by a river of frequencies that come from death, the flesh and hell.

Let us look at the following illustration, which will show how our spirit and our soul operate amongst the two currents that constantly influence them.

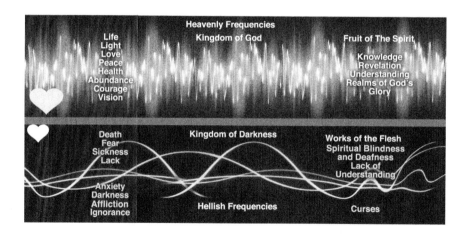

Figure 33 - Heavenly and Hellish Frequencies

with their respective fruits

Here we see the fruit of the Spirit and the glorious riches in Christ reflected, versus the works of the flesh and its consequences.

Now the works of the flesh are evident, which are: adultery, fornication, uncleanness, lewdness,

idolatry, sorcery, hatred, contentions, jealousies, outbursts of wrath, selfish ambitions, dissensions, heresies,

envy, murders, drunkenness, revelries, and the like; of which I tell you beforehand, just as I also told you in time past, that those who practice such things will not inherit the kingdom of God.

But the fruit of the Spirit is love, joy, peace, longsuffering, kindness, goodness, faithfulness,

Gentleness, self-control. Against such there is no law.

And those who are Christ's have crucified the flesh with its passions and desires.

If we live in the Spirit, let us also walk in the Spirit.

Galatians 5:19-25

When the spirit is reigning over the soul, our spiritual life will grow.

Jesus Christ is the life, and life is the light of men. The more life of Jesus I have in me, the more light will be manifested. Light is the frequency of heaven, and has the highest frequency of vibration in the entire universe.

But the path of the just is like the shining sun that shines ever brighter unto the perfect day.

Proverbs 4:18

This light grows more and more intense, opening up for us the way of revelation, understanding and knowledge of God, and to the glorious dimensions of His Kingdom.

Light is His manifested love, His peace, and the indescribable joy of being in Him and Him in us. The more we remain in the high frequencies of the Spirit, the healthier we will be, since sickness cannot penetrate the Kingdom of God.

People remain sick because they seek answers in the low frequencies of this world. They then grow eager and are filled with fear, so the healing that awaits them in the higher frequencies never reaches them.

When we feel sick, instead of running to the doctor, we can quiet down the low voices of the soul and allow faith, which comes from the spirit, to raise our frequency[24].

Perhaps, you need to find a moment when you don't have much pain or symptoms and use this time to lift up your soul and immerse it in the levels of the Spirit.

Find the peace that comes from the Lord Jesus. Begin to project your love towards Him and exalt Him, because there is nothing impossible for Him. Analyze your soul in the light of His justice and thank Him because He took all your sickness to the cross.

Peace attracts the Kingdom of Heaven, its angels and its answers. Worry and fear attract the kingdom of darkness and its tormenting spirits.

---

[24] To depend on God and not the doctors, depends on the faith of each person and their walk with God. We don't recommend stopping medication or seeing doctors for people who do not hear the voice of God telling them to do so. Voice of The Light Ministries is not responsible for the decision each person makes in respect to this.

The frequencies of heaven will also attract abundance to your life; great amounts of valuable and honorable people to surround you, as well as an abundance of assets, so that you can live like the son of a King and be generous in every good work.

> *Arise, shine; for your light has come! And the glory of the Lord is risen upon you.*
>
> *For behold, the darkness shall cover the earth, and deep darkness the people; but the Lord will arise over you, and His glory will be seen upon you.*
>
> *Then you shall see and become radiant, and your heart shall swell with joy; because the abundance of the sea shall be turned to you, the wealth of the Gentiles shall come to you.*
>
> *Isaiah 60:1-2; 5*

> *It is the Spirit who gives life; the flesh profits nothing. The words that I speak to you are spirit, and they are life.*
>
> *John 6:63*

The flesh, which comes from the soul, the world and its rudiments are useless. Not only that, they bring lack, anguish, sickness, ignorance, fears and disgrace.

In this illustration, we see the heart being not constant in its process of development to reach the full measure of the Spirit. There are moments when it manages to raise itself to high spheres and enters the frequencies of God, but then descends to low frequencies where it is used to living.

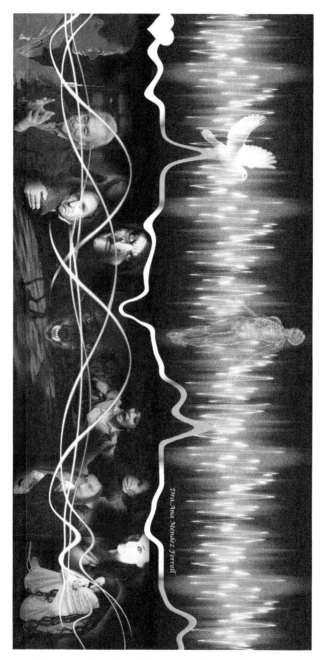

Figure 34 - The Heart oscillating between

the Heavenly and Hellish Frequencies

We see in the illustration from left to right, the dependency on medicine, human science, greed, financial fears, witchcraft, demonic oppression, terror, religion (in any of its forms), seduction and depression. We could add to this list everything that implies living under the principles and ways of this world.

Above, we see the frequencies of heaven trying to take the heart to the presence of God, to being committed to Him and to elevate the spirit to the dimensions of light.

When we see this, we realize why the Word of God condemns friendship with the world so much.

Adulterers and adulteresses! Do you not know that friendship with the world is enmity with God? Whoever therefore wants to be a friend of the world makes himself an enemy of God.

James 4:4

It is our responsibility to learn and detect low frequencies and come out of them as soon as we realize they are dragging us down, grabbing hold of us or tying us up. Sometimes it will imply a tremendous battle between the spirit and the soul, until we obtain total victory.

Low frequencies are not insignificant; they have kept humanity captive for thousands of years. They are like waves of water that drown the soul to keep it within everything that is death. What we have to understand is that high frequencies will always dominate the low ones; the same way light dominates darkness because God and the devil are not equal in strength in any way.

To know this in our heart is the power to come out of them.

The sorrows of Sheol surrounded me; the snares of death confronted me.

In my distress I called upon the Lord, and cried out to my God; He heard my voice from His temple, and my cry came before Him, even to His ears.

He sent from above, He took me; He drew me from many waters.

He delivered me from my strong enemy, from those who hated me, for they were too strong for me.

Psalms 18:5-6; 16-17

PART IV

INTERRELATION
OF THE SPIRIT,
SOUL AND BODY

Chapter 12

INTERRELATION OF THE TRIPARTITE BEING

Our entire being: spirit, soul and body are intimately related in all its parts.

We are the temple of the Spirit in our integral composition. Therefore, the way the natural body is assembled is similar to how the spiritual is put together.

> *... vainly puffed up by his fleshly mind,*
>
> *and not holding fast to the Head, from whom all the body, nourished and knit together by joints and ligaments, grows with the increase that is from God.*
>
> *Colossians 2:18b; 19*

Each one of the components of the spirit has its equivalent in the soul. These two connect with the body through joints and ligaments, which either transfer the life of the spirit, or death through the unregenerate soul.

When we studied the soul, we discussed these interconnections and how the ligaments between the spiritual and natural mind are atrophied as long as the soul does not regenerate.

We also saw how the heart is divided into two ventricles, one of the spirit and one of the soul, and how they function.

We will now see how much the condition of our spirit, as well as the soul, will have a great influence on the body and will determine its condition.

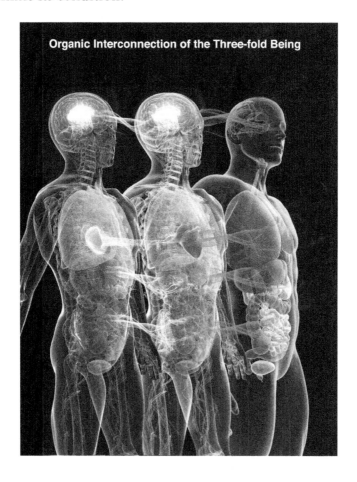

Fig. 35 Organic Interconnection of the Tripartite Being

Science has understood a part of this, and refers to diseases that have no pathological explanation as psychosomatic. That is, they do not find a single external agent such as a virus or bacteria or organic atrophy, which causes the sickness.

The world and its philosophies have also understood that a healthy mind produces a healthy body. New age tries to harmonize the body with the universe and with the earth. Oriental religions state that there is a relation between the spirit of man and his physical condition. These are all fragments of knowledge that man has tried to understand in his fallen soul. The truth is only the Creator of our tripartite being can give us the complete picture through the Holy Spirit's revelation.

When our spirit, united with God, has the supremacy to govern over our being, the soul is flooded with the life of God, the same as the body. This leads to a life of peace and perfect health. In the same way, the soul with its deformities and conflicts also has an effect on our health.

Let us now see how our human body is affected by the condition of our invisible being.

1. The Process of Sickness

While Adam and his wife were in the Garden of Eden, sickness and death did not exist. As a matter of fact, when God told them if they ate from the tree of good and evil they would die, this was an unimaginable concept to them, since they did not know what that meant.

When the first man and woman lost their garments of immortality, which are Christ, their spirit not only fell into a dormant state, but it was exposed to darkness. They were thrown out of the environment of light and out from the protection of

God, and entered a dark world where death and satan had dominion.

They experienced the loss of a loved one and saw a dead body for the first time when Cain slew Abel. The Fear of death entered their hearts in that moment, and enslaved them to the plans of their adversary.

> *Inasmuch then as the children have partaken of flesh and blood, He Himself likewise shared in the same, that through death He might destroy him who had the power of death, that is, the devil,*
>
> *and release those who through fear of death were all their lifetime subject to bondage.*
>
> *Hebrews 2:14-15*

A. Sickness that comes from the Inside

All sickness begins with the condition of the spirit. Adam lived in perfect health up until the moment when death entered his spirit. From that point on, organs began to decay, age and atrophy until he died.

Notice that mortality and sickness did not enter through a virus or through natural causes, but through the spirit of man, which lost his state of perfection, united with God.

That is why it is so important to be "born again" and take the time to be in communion with God, so that life in its strongest form can invade our bodies once again.

For since by man came death, by Man also came the resurrection of the dead.

For as in Adam all die, even so in Christ all shall be made alive.

1 Corinthians 15:21-22

1. Darkness needs the Soul to sicken the Body

The fall not only affected man, but also the earth, which suffered the effects of the change in spiritual government. It was filled with curses and darkness, and even its aspect changed, filling itself with thorns and thistles. I believe even the colors changed and became dull and earthy. This goes to show that the natural world is affected by the spiritual world.

satan, who is the defeated prince of lies and deceit, leads darkness and death. Darkness is by definition the absence of light, and as a result, has no substance. There are no atoms of darkness or anything that can physically measure it, like energy and light are measured.

satan relies on tricks to penetrate the physical world, and man's soul becomes very useful to him for this end.

God gave man the power over life and death in his tongue, which speaks what he determines and believes.

Death and life are in the power of the tongue, and those who love it will eat its fruit.

Proverbs 18:21

When a spirit receives salvation and has been partially awakened by the Seed of Life, it still has a great amount of death and iniquity which has to be purged.

That is why we see so many faithful and sincere Sons of God who are still fighting for their health. Being unaware of the truth does not exempt us from the consequences.

As we saw when we studied "the inheritance" or spiritual genetics, iniquity is transferred from the spirit to the soul and then into the body.

> *As he clothed himself with cursing as with his garment,*
> *so let it enter his body like water,*
>
> *Psalms 109:18*

We clearly see in this scripture how something spiritual, like a curse, transforms into actual physical matter, which, manifests in the body.

> *No one calls for justice, nor does any plead for truth.*
> *They trust in empty words and speak lies; they conceive*
> *evil and bring forth iniquity.*
>
> *They hatch vipers' eggs and weave the spider's web; he*
> *who eats of their eggs dies, and from that which is*
> *crushed a viper breaks out.*
>
> *Isaiah 59:4-5*

We also see the work of iniquity veiling the understanding of the people in this scripture; even believers, who take justice into their own hands, bring judgment on others, and trust more in man, his solutions and science, than they do in God. To conceive evil does not necessarily mean committing a crime; everything that does not come from the heart of God and is not aligned to His will is evil. Does God not say in scripture that our righteousness is like filthy rags (Isaiah 64:6)?

Unfortunately, the majority of people have settled for crumbs from heaven, when God has given us all the bread of life to live by Him.

All of this evil produces asp eggs, which translate into tumors and cancers. They weave spider webs that contaminate the entire lymphatic and immunological system. People run to the doctor in search of answers so that he can provide them a chemical remedy for something that has its origin in the spirit, or in the soul.

As we saw earlier, iniquity comes from the spirit and directly contaminates the natural mind and the heart within the soul. Once it settles on the soul, it enters as negative energy through the lymphatic, nervous and endocrine systems. The endocrine system controls the glands and the hormones in the body and is the chemical factory of our body.

For example, let us look at iniquity resulting from racial hate. The soul receives this hate from the spirit and translates it into racial imaginations and thoughts. The natural mind sends these signals to the brain, where the pituitary and hypothalamus glands release negative amino acids throughout the body. These amino acids are secretions that penetrate into the bloodstream and get to the cells where they sicken or destroy them.

People filled with hate, resentment and bitterness will find that their kidneys, liver and spleen, the filters of the body, will be gravely affected.

Others that do not let go of their pain and cannot forgive or are stingy will suffer from arthritis. Their joints start to deform, reflecting the spiritual condition of someone that retains his pain or his possessions.

The body reflects the condition of the spirit!

Blood diseases are directly related to blood shedding, wars, abortion, blood covenants in witchcraft or Freemasonry and homicide. This could all be a part of the spiritual inheritance from our ancestors that has not been purged from the spirit.

Cardiac problems have to do with unresolved emotional suffering.

Respiratory problems have to do with spirits of darkness; these are made out of an airy substance controlled by the prince of the power of the air. Air gives us life and is rather related to God, or to what we depend on. These diseases are related to idolatry and witchcraft, dependence on man before God, religious attitudes and spirits that take the place of God in our soul.

Cancer consists of rebellious cells that multiply and refuse to be a part of the organism as God created it. This is obviously linked to rebellion and a desire to be independent and self-sufficient. It is also linked to divisions and to building one's own kingdom and not the Kingdom of God.

God states in His word, that bones dry up due to sadness and iniquity. Obesity not only comes from overeating, but from a spirit that accumulates possessions. In a lot of cases we see these people's closets filled with clutter they will never use. They lease warehouses to continue storing things they do not need, and this is the message they are transferring onto their own body.

We can continue breaking down disease by disease and search what they mean in the spirit.

Observe people's faces. As they age, they begin to transform into the image of their own spirit. Those that practice witchcraft have the face of a witch. Mean people look evil. All sin is made visible sooner or later in the body or in the person's appearance.

2. Health comes from Within

On the other hand, health, which comes from the flow of life within the seat of communion, takes the same route to restore our bodies.

God is the Life, transmitted to all spirits, because we are all His. He is the Father of all spirits. He is always transmitting His vital energy to the spirit of every man and from there to the soul and body otherwise we would die. So whether our spirit is dormant or awake, or whether we are believers or not, we will receive our health from Him.

Even doctors know that a positive attitude, a desire to be healed and the faith to believe it, helps the recuperation process. On the contrary, a nervous and fearful person that always thinks the worst will aggravate the situation.

In the following illustration we see the spirit in the central figure, transmitting health to the nervous and lymphatic systems through the mind of the spirit and the heart's valve. This same signal comes from the brain and penetrates the endocrine system as well as the glands in the zone of the brain. Then life transmits positive thoughts of health to the mind of the soul. The mind of the soul will then transmit them to the brain, where the nervous system will then send the signal to the endocrine system. Once the impulse is received in the glands, they will produce positive peptides or amino acids that flow through the bloodstream and get to the cells to regenerate them.

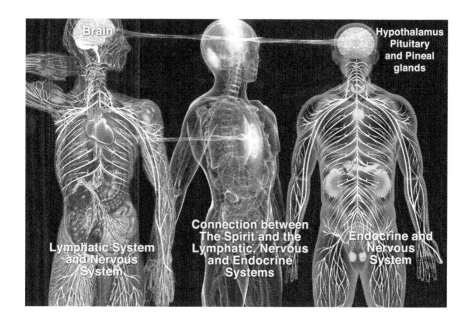

Figure 36 - Health System: The Spirit Sending the Flow of Life

to the Heart and the Brain.

3. Plexuses, Glands and Lymphatic Nodules

In order to deeply understand the process of sickness and health that comes from within, we will analyze several important components. The spirit and soul connects to our body through three main systems, which are all interconnected. These are the nervous system, glandular or endocrine system and the lymphatic system.

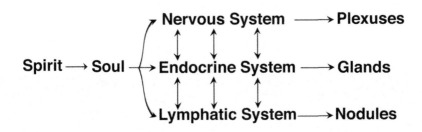

Interlinked Systems with the Spirit and the Soul

Figure 37 - Interconnected Systems and

their Spirit-Soul Components

a. The Nervous System and its Plexuses

There are certain areas in this system where there is a great concentration of nerves, which science has referred to as plexuses. When we hear this word we automatically think of the solar plexus so commonly used by those involved in New Age. However, this is not an esoteric term, but rather a biological word. Further, there are others like the cardiac plexus, the aortic plexus, sub mucosal and others.

Some of these plexuses are linked to the center of emotions and the heart of the soul. That is why we feel our heart hurts when we experience a strong offense or the loss of a loved one. We have also experienced butterflies in our stomach when we are very excited or we withdraw inside of us when we feel fear. All of this has to do with the conglomeration of nerves that are connected to our soul.

Further ahead we will see how some of these plexuses are true spiritual doors to the Kingdom of God and also into that of darkness.

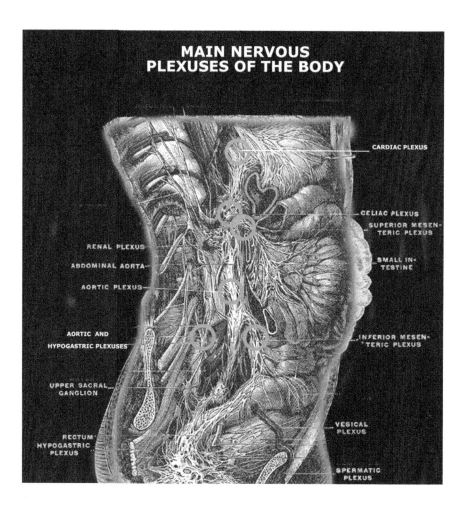

Figure 38 - The Most Important Plexuses in the Nervous System

b. The Lymphatic System

The lymphatic system is the body's energy conductor. The anointing of God flows through it from the spirit to all the organs. It is, so to speak, a network of highways through which God's light travels throughout our bodies.

These avenues are blocked due to iniquity and the death substances it produces, as well as by the toxins we consume.

The lymphatic nodules are like small bags that are found all along the lymphatic conduits and are joined to some of the nerve plexuses and to the glands of the endocrine system.

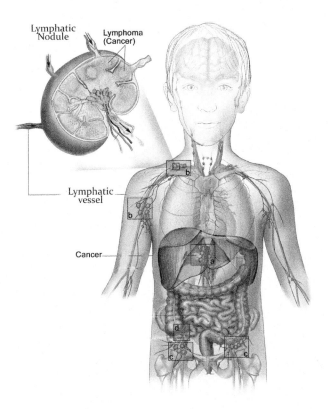

Figure 39 - Lymphatic Nodules

One of the most important lymphatic glands is called "Thymus." This one regulates and controls the flow of energy. It corrects the imbalances as soon as they are detected to obtain the utmost balance of energy in the body. This gland connects directly with the mind of the soul, being the first organ affected by mental stress.

The lymphatic system also breaks down toxins turning them harmless before they enter into the bloodstream and into the liver and kidneys. It can also cast them directly out from the body, through perspiration.

The lymphatic conduits are found just underneath the skin and the lymph is the transparent liquid that oozes when we have a wound. The lymphatic glands are located in the neck, the underarms and the groin and often swell when there is an infection.

Further ahead when we study the process of sickness that comes from outside, we will see how the lymphatic system plays a very important role in our health.

c. The Endocrine System

This system is our body's pharmacy. The fundamental pieces of this system are hormones and glands. Serving as chemical messengers of the body, hormones transmit information and instructions among the cells. Even though many different types of hormones circulate through the bloodstream, each type is designed to only affect certain cells. The glands are responsible to produce hormones and amino acids and transfer them to the lymphatic system and to the bloodstream.

The endocrine system is linked to our soul and is one of the systems the enemy longs to control. The secretion of certain hormones or the lack thereof will affect our mood. This is something very enticing for the enemy to use to bring out certain behaviors that will lead him to victory over a particular soul.

It is very easy to observe the mood swings of a woman during menstruation. Many become depressed, others become angry, and some become very sensitive being offended at everything.

I became a very happy woman when God taught me how to separate my endocrine system from my emotions by simply making a declaration: "In the name of the Lord Jesus Christ, I voluntarily separate my emotions and my heart from my endocrine system. It will never again control my mood." Since then, my emotions have never been affected by hormonal change.

B. Sickness that comes from the Outside

Not all sickness comes from the inside. The prince of darkness, whose objective is to steal, kill and destroy, sends diseases to afflict and kill man.

Some people think that God sends diseases to deal with them, but that is not the nature of God.

For I know the thoughts that I think toward you, says the Lord, thoughts of peace and not of evil, to give you a future and a hope.

Jeremiah 29:11

Every good gift and every perfect gift is from above, and comes down from the Father of lights, with whom there is no variation or shadow of turning.

James 1:17

Suffering Job lived in a time very different from today. At the time, Jesus had not yet taken our diseases on the cross and satan had not been cast out of his position as the accuser.

Jesus paid an immeasurable price so that we could live in perfect health, not to send us sicknesses, which are part of the kingdom of death.

Inasmuch then as the children have partaken of flesh and blood, He Himself likewise shared in the same, that through death He might destroy him who had the power of death, that is, the devil,

Hebrews 2:14

A son of God becomes sick because of what he determines to believe in his heart.

1. The Attack begins in the Spirit of Man

In order to get to the soul, the devil must penetrate through the spirit since he is a spiritual being without a soul.

The first thing he will do is send a certain disease in the form of oppression and darkness over an area of the spirit (see the following illustration).

Up until that moment it is nothing but a lie from darkness and has no substance. However, the lie has a certain amount of power in the way it operates causing man to believe it.

The oppression sent to the spirit, acts as a symptom in the body, which begins to manifest as discomfort or pain.

Once the body receives the lying signals sent in the form of illness, the mind accepts them. More than likely, the person will go see a doctor, who will confirm that what is being felt, is real, and that indeed the person has a sickness.

Fear comes down into the heart, which believes this beyond a reasonable doubt, and the tongue, which has the power to give life or death, confesses the disease.

In that moment, what started out as a lie in the spirit realm manifests into actual matter in the physical body, and truly sickens the body.

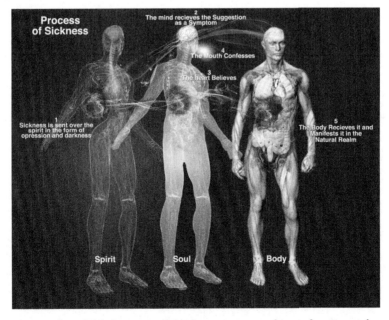

Figure 40 - The Process of Sickness sent in from the Outside

The first attack has been successful and now the devil sends in his second onslaught: to destroy the body through chemical medication, which is full of side effects.

The damage will first be against the defense system, which is found within the lymphatic system. The lymph (lymphatic liquid) and the lymphatic nodules will be filled with chemical toxins, which will inhibit the production of antibodies. The lymphatic system is the dumpster of the body and its function is to eliminate toxins so that they will not affect the rest of the organism. Once the organs are weakened by pharmaceuticals they are unprotected, and the assault of the devil will then be without mercy. To put it simply, the offensive strategy is to do away with the army of defense that God placed inside of us, which is in fact VERY POWERFUL. Once the guard is brought down, the chemicals will block the excretion of toxins through the sudoriferous glands (sweat glands). This will create an environment prone to sickness in the entire organism.

The lymphatic glands produce a substance called lymphocytes, which is the body's defense mechanism. These reach all tissue becoming the primary defense against sickness.

The ancient Greeks considered the Thymus gland extremely important, and called it THUMOS. In Greek it means: Soul, or Life, because it is situated in the center of the chest, close to the places where emotions are felt and very close to the physical heart. An active and healthy Thymus Gland contributes to good health and a strong immune system.

2. Oppression and Pain

The devil uses weapons and instruments of torture to bring oppression and discomfort to our bodies. He sends them to the spirit the same way he sends sickness.

These manifest as sharp pain located in particular parts of the body; generally in the neck, shoulders, the waist and the head.

Above all, taking the shield of faith with which you will be able to quench all the fiery darts of the wicked one.

Ephesians 6:16

No weapon formed against you shall prosper, and every tongue, which rises against you in judgment, you shall condemn. This is the heritage of the servants of the Lord, and their righteousness is from Me," says the Lord.

Isaiah 54:17

People generally try to treat the pain with painkillers, massages or other natural remedies, but these are useless or of little effect, since the problem originated in the spirit.

Doctors, finding nothing in their diagnoses, call this fibromyalgia, migraines, et cetera and fill people with drugs.

In the illustrations, I placed some instruments of torture that are used, which we have identified when praying for people or for our own bodies.

There are presses with which the devil squeezes the head or back. He also uses sarcophaguses and belts with nails, daggers, hooks, collars with spikes, asphyxiating masks, and thick spider webs which he places in the frontal and nasal passages, shoes with sharp objects inside of them, and animal traps, et cetera.

Even though this sounds terrible, the truth is they are very easy to treat. The eyes of our spirit are equipped with the ability to see these weapons that are launched against us. The more we exercise this, the easier it will be to see them. Once we locate the weapon, remove it as if you were seeing it physically. Keep in mind that certain knives have very sharp teeth, which we cannot just remove in one yank. The same goes for hooks.

If you don't see this clearly, ask the Holy Spirit to reveal what weapons are used and then remove them.

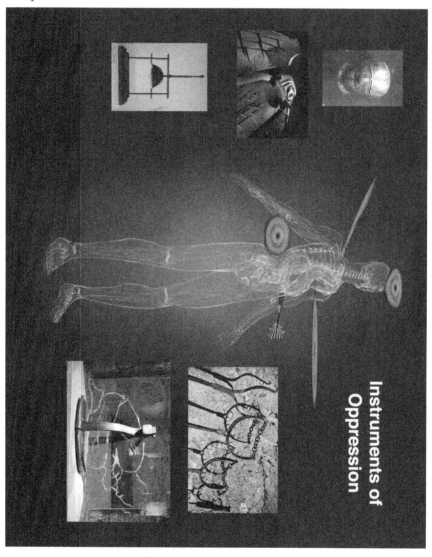

Figure 41 - Instruments of Oppression

3. Jesus paid for our Sickness

It is important that every one whose spirit has been born of God knows that He paid the price for all sickness and that we can all live in perfect health. Sometimes there will be attacks since the devil hates us, but we do not have to succumb to them.

... Resist the devil and he will flee from you.

James 4:7

...And said, "If you diligently heed the voice of the Lord your God and do what is right in His sight, give ear to His commandments and keep all His statutes, I will put none of the diseases on you which I have brought on the Egyptians. For I am the Lord who heals you."

Exodus 15:26

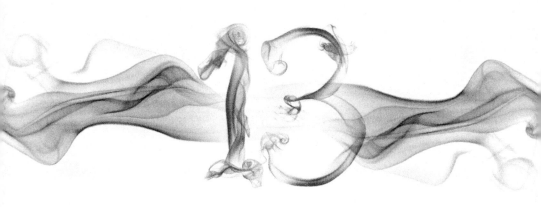

Chapter 13

THE DOORS OF THE SPIRIT

In the previous chapter we analyzed how the three systems, lymphatic, endocrine and nervous, are interconnected. We will now see how they unite with the soul and the spirit.

1. The Doors of a Redeemed Spirit

Once our spirit has been born again into the Kingdom of God, it has converted into the tabernacle where He dwells.

During the Babylonian captivity, God gave Prophet Ezekiel the design of a temple that was never built. Even though these are the plans of a physical building in the old covenant, they have a lot to do with our spiritual building. Even the way he received this vision is very useful to us when it comes to understanding the different aspects of our spirit.

And the Lord said to me, "Son of man, mark well, see with your eyes and hear with your ears, all that I say to you concerning all the ordinances of the house of the Lord and all its laws. **Mark well who may enter the house and all who go out from the sanctuary***.*

Ezekiel 44:5

In Chapter 4, we studied the "silver cord", and saw in the scripture how God gives man the ability to be taken to different spiritual and physical places.

In order for this to take place, the spirit goes out through the doors the Lord designed in our spiritual being.

One of the main doors is found in the upper part of the head. That is why the laying on of hands to impart a spiritual gift or to anoint a minister is done in this part of our body.

He stretched out the form of a hand, **and took me by a lock of my hair***; and the Spirit lifted me up between earth and heaven, and brought me in visions of God to Jerusalem, to the door of the north gate of the inner court, where the seat of the image of jealousy was, which provokes to jealousy.*

Ezekiel 8:3

Another important door is found in the back of the neck, also referred to as the occipital, where the head is joined to the neck.

A third door is found by the valve of the spirit, at the height of the solar and cardiac plexuses. Finally, a fourth is found in the center of the brain, uniting the pineal gland and optical plexuses.

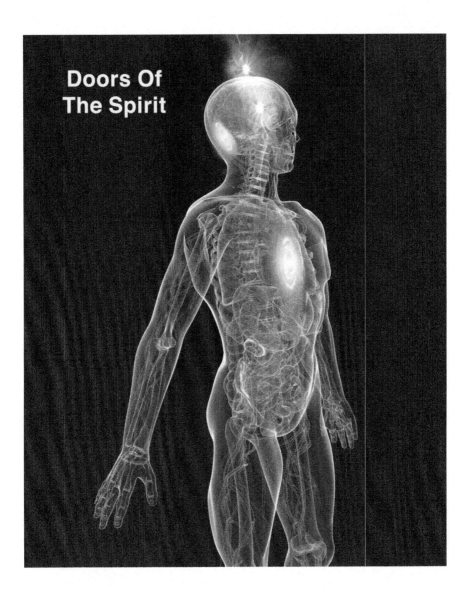

Figure 42 - The Doors of the Spirit

All four doors serve as entrances to receive visions and impartations from the Spirit of God, but only two have access to the outside; the one on the upper part of the head, and the one close to the valve.

> *In the visions of God He took me into the land of Israel and set me on a very high mountain; on it toward the south was something like the structure of a city.*
>
> *And the man said to me, "Son of man, look with your eyes and hear with your ears, and fix your mind on everything I show you;* **for you were brought here** *so that I might show them to you."*
>
> *Ezekiel 40:2; 4a*

Disgracefully, the enemy has used these doors as well as others that lead to the soul and body, to infiltrate himself within the human being to oppress him and even possessing him.

A great amount of believers, as well as non-believers, being unaware of these entrances find themselves under terrible yokes and do not know how to deal with them.

> *He who digs a pit will fall into it, and whoever breaks through a wall will be bitten by a serpent.*
>
> *Ecclesiastes 10:8*

When doors are ignored, danger is eminent. That is why it is important to understand how the enemy uses them. When someone has been involved in the occult or in the New Age, they have opened doors that must be closed.

The confessing of sins is not enough to close them; it has to be a conscious act on our part. Our ancestors could have been the ones opening these doors, causing us to be born with open and contaminated doors.

Let us look at what some of these doors are.

2. The enemy's usurped and created Doors

The devil, to whom man gave dominion over creation after the fall, has been very astute in deceiving man, especially when it comes to spiritual matters.

He has made man believe that by simply developing his mental and spiritual abilities, he can connect to what he has called "the great universal mind".

In all experiences inspired by the fallen angel of light, he will ensure that guardians are invited to guide man in those experiences.

These guardians are demonic spirits that disguise themselves using "godly names" so ignorant people would fall in the trap. God is the only one that can take man into heavenly places through the Holy Spirit. If man attempts an astral projection, without the help of a spiritual entity he will simply die. These guardian spirits maintain the connection between the body and the spirit so that the person can travel.

In order for this to take place, these guardians must have access to the doors of the spirit. Some examples that will help you understand this concept, are being presented by Hollywood in the last decades.

The movie "*Avatar*" clearly shows these doors. For those who have understanding, it is a very revealing movie about the doctrines the devil wants to establish on the earth. The magical world where the avatars move about is the spiritual world created by Satan. Every character has an analog "I," that looks like them, and represents their spiritual being in that dimension. In order to be transported, they utilize dragons, which in reality are spiritual guardians in charge of taking them on astral projections. Avatars are joined to the dragons by connecting their braided hair unto an elongated appendix that comes out of the dragon's head. The point of contact between the dragon and the avatar is the occipital door of the spirit, which is found between the cranium and the neck.

Figure 43 "Avatar" - Connected to the Dragon

His braid comes from the occipital region and penetrates the tubular appendix of the animal.

In other movies like "*The Matrix*", we also see that in order to enter the other dimension, they must be connected in that same area.

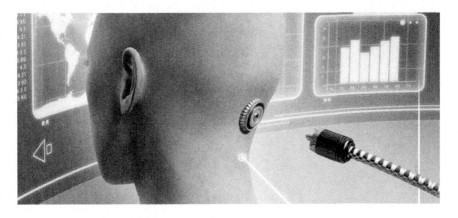

Figure 44 - Connection used in "The Matrix"

and other digital Games

This door is directly connected to the pineal gland in the center of the brain. Demonic spirits or dead people's ghosts that spiritualists invoke enter and exit through this door.

The devil also uses this door to send all kinds of pornographic and terror images to the screen of the spirit. It is the door he uses to infiltrate and bring in disturbing dreams and nightmares.

satan will also use the body's energy centers, located in the main glands. He does this to open doors and control the soul and its appetites, since he knows the glands determine a great amount of man's physical and emotional health.

He calls these doors "chakras", which means circles in Sanskrit. These are wheels of active energy. The devil activates these wheels of energy, and with practice, they begin to transform into funnels, which he uses to introduce his spirits.

Figure 45 - Demonic Doors

These energy centers or demonic doors are interconnected with the soul in the soulish ventricle of the heart and with the spirit in the seat of iniquity. The spirits of darkness and their destructive energy travel through a pathway created by the devil within the soul of the person called: "The Kundalini Serpent" that runs down the spinal cord. This serpent itself is connected to a dragon in the spiritual universe called "Ouroboros."

If we analyze our body, we will see the main endocrine glands converge with the nerve plexuses and lymphatic glands. It is precisely at these points of union where the connections to the soul and the spirit are produced. That is why there is such a great deal of energy concentrated in the nerve plexuses.

As I said before, the devil is very interested in our glands, since they control a great deal of man's moods. Establishing his doors there will give him the ability to control sexuality and destructive emotions, such as anxiety, anger, depression, et cetera. Let us see how these doors have been established precisely where these three systems converge and are strongly connected to the soul and spirit.

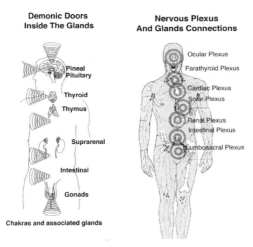

Figure 46 - Correlation Between Demonic Doors,
Endocrine Glands and Nerve Plexuses

These doors are also used to transfer spirits from one person to another, and they are also used to release spiritual energy and demonic spirits to a certain place. The door on the upper part of the head is the seat of government, where the devil will position himself to completely control a person involved in spiritual practices outside of God. It is also used to connect people with the demonic spiritual realm. Many are deceived because this is a fallen angel that knew heaven. He shows them fragments of heavenly places that he re-created. He is an expert illusionist, capable of re-creating all kinds scenarios in order to deceive.

Followers of many religions and occultist practices are instructed to cover their heads as an act of protecting the sacred area of their spirit, where the presence of their god sits. They don't do this as an act of reverence; they know it is a spiritual door and a seat of power. We see this in Voodoo, Santeria, Hinduism, Catholicism and in many others.

With time the people who practice in opening these doors suffers from cardiac arrest, abdominal pains, glandular and cerebral problems, among many others.

It is important to close these doors from our past or from our heritage. In this manner, God can use the true doors He put in our spirit without any danger of infiltration.

3. Closing evil Doors and opening God's Doors

Closing doors is very easy, whether you opened them yourself, or were born with open doors due to certain practices initiated by your ancestors.

If you wish, you may pray this prayer with me with all of your heart, believing in what you are doing:

"Heavenly Father, I come before you in the name of Jesus Christ, and I ask for your forgiveness for opening these doors and for my ancestors that opened them. I renounce every guardian spirit that has entered through them, as well as the Kundalini serpent and the Ouroboros, the dragon. I command them to leave my life and the life of my generations."

Now, placing your hand on each one of the chakras, as well as the door that is found in the lower part of the back of the neck, say:

"Of my own free will I close this door forever with an iron lock and it will never again be used by the devil or his spirits. I disconnect all ties the devil has made, uniting these connections with my spirit, soul, glands and lymphatic and nervous systems. I renounce the energy of darkness and sickness that was established in my organs through these doors, and I command it to come out of my life, in the name of Jesus, King of Kings.

I now place the blood of Jesus Christ in each one of the doors and I consecrate them to the Heavenly Father."

Now place your hand in the 4 doors that were created by God within you (see Figure 45 - Doors of the Spirit) and declare the following:

"I declare the doors of my spirit belong only to God in His three persons: Father, Son and Holy Spirit, and they remain completely consecrated in His hands, to be used only by Him in my spiritual development. I thank Him for creating me to be the extraordinary being I now know I am. I ask Lord, that You show me through Your Spirit, to live according to You, and not according to the flesh and it's reasoning. I renounce the tree of the knowledge of good and evil and all of its principles, and I receive the tree of life, which is the flow of the life of the Spirit of God, united with mine. In the Name of the Lord Jesus Christ, Amen."

Do this in each door and use olive oil, or aromatic oil, declaring that it is the symbol of the Holy Spirit, and apply it to every door you closed.

If you have never made a covenant of salvation with the Heavenly Father to consecrate yourself to Him completely, and recognize Jesus Christ as your Lord and Savior, it is important that you do so. There are no neutral zones in the spiritual world.

You either belong to the kingdom of Light or to the kingdom of darkness.

If this is your desire and you wish to reach the fullness narrated in this book, open your heart, and ask God for forgiveness of all your sins.

Feel the repentance necessary so that the foreskin is removed from your heart. Yearn for salvation with all of your soul, and ask the Lord Jesus, the Father and the Spirit, in your own words to come and live in your heart. Ask Him to take possession of your golden bowl and to make His dwelling in your heart.

May God bless you abundantly and develop a powerful spirit within you to establish the Kingdom of God on the Earth. My prayer is that you will be seen as the true lineage of Yahweh (Jehovah) full of power, wisdom and holiness; a true son or daughter of God that makes a difference on the earth.

The End

Participate in our
On Demand Courses

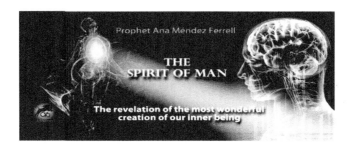

www.virtualata.com

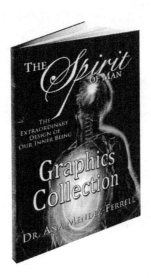

You can watch us online

on our channel

Frequencies of Glory TV

Powerful messages and worship

www.frequenciesofglorytv.com

 Follow us on Facebook

Voice Of The Light
Ministries

www.voiceofthelight.com

904-834-2447

P.O. Box 3418

Ponte Vedra, FL. 32004

USA

Printed in Great Britain
by Amazon

30486334R00136